Bearbeitungsklappe
(Editing Flap)

Kate Pelling

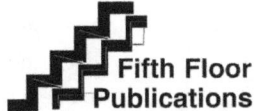
Fifth Floor
Publications

Bearbeitungsklappe [Editing Flap]
By Kate Pelling
Published by Fifth Floor Publications,
London, UK and Frankfurt am Main, Germany
Copyright 2016 Fifth Floor Publications and
Kate Pelling

ISBN 978-0-9576128-2-2

Bearbeitungsklappe [Editing Flap]
von Kate Pelling
Verlegt durch Fifth Floor Publications,
London, Großbritannien und Frankfurt am
Main, Deutschland
Copyright 2016 Fifth Floor Publications und
Kate Pelling

ISBN 978-0-9576128-2-2

CONTENTS/INHALTSVERZEICHNIS:

INTRODUCTION

This publication is a book of drawings. It is also a piece of experimental video art. Of course 'experimental' covers a wide range of artistic practice, but a common definition of experimental film and video is 'film-making without story, characters or plot – or in which these elements, considered so essential to cinematic form, are put into new and critical relationships' (Rees, 1999, p. vi). This publication puts forward a new and critical relationship relating to editing practices, by expanding the language and strategies available for editing experimental film and video. A. L. Rees also described the field as 'allied to painting, sculpture, printmaking and other arts both traditional and modern' (1999, p. vii). In this book, experimental video, drawing, text and the process of publication are more than just allies – they are brought together in a transdisciplinary approach to editing video. Transdisciplinary *'concerns the transfer of methods from one discipline to another'* and involves

EINLEITUNG

Das vorliegende Buch besteht aus Zeichnungen. Zugleich ist es aber auch ein experimentelles Videokunstwerk. Freilich deckt der Begriff „experimentell" eine große Bandbreite von künstlerischen Praktiken ab. Laut einer allgemeinen Definition haben experimentelle Filme und Videos keine „Geschichte, Darsteller oder Handlung - oder setzen diese Elemente, die für die Filmform als wesentlich angesehen werden, in neue und kritische Verhältnisse" (Rees, 1999, Seite vi). Dieses Werk bietet eine neue und kritische Perspektive auf die Praktiken des Editierens, indem es Sprache und Strategien, die zur Bearbeitung von experimentellem Film und Video zur Verfügung stehen, erweitert. A. L. Rees beschrieb diesen Bereich auch als „verbunden mit Malerei, Bildhauerei, Drucken und weiteren, sowohl traditionellen als auch modernen Kunstformen" (1999, Seite vii). In diesem Buch sind experimentelles Video, Zeichnung, Text

being 'at once between the disciplines, across the different disciplines and beyond all disciplines' (Nicolescu, 2008, p. 2). So this is a book of drawings, and a piece of experimental video art, and also between, across and beyond these disciplines.

The ninety-five drawings within these pages have resulted from editing a video that was recorded through the letterbox of my house in Niederbrechen, Germany, over a period of nine hours on the 30th March 2015. The title of this publication refers to the letterbox ('Editing Flap'), because it begins the editing process by limiting the scope of what the camera could record. Twenty-four 'events' took place within this time/letterbox frame, such as people returning from the shops, cars transporting their owners to work, or a cat going about its daily business. The drawings in this publication show edited versions of these twenty-four events, with each comprising of between two and five drawings. In some cases, the multiple editing processes take the image very far away from the original point of recording. The final stage of the editing process is publication, where the drawings are brought together and put into an order, not in a chronological sequence but as a narrative staging of the events that reflects ideas that

und der Bearbeitungsprozess mehr als nur miteinander verbunden - sie werden in einem transdisziplinären Ansatz zur Videobearbeitung zusammengebracht. Transdisziplinarität „betrifft den Transfer von Methoden von einer Disziplin zu einer anderen" sowie „zur gleichen Zeit zwischen den Disziplinen, über die verschiedenen Disziplinen und über alle Disziplinen hinaus zu sein" (Nicolescu, 2008, Seite 2). Somit stellt dieses Werk ein Buch mit Zeichnungen und ein experimentelles Videokunstwerk dar, zugleich bewegt es sich auch zwischen den Disziplinen, durch diese und über sie hinaus.

Die 95 Zeichnungen auf diesen Seiten sind das Ergebnis der Bearbeitung eines Videos, das in einem Zeitraum von neun Stunden am 30. März 2015 durch den Briefeinwurfschlitz meines Hauses in Niederbrechen in Deutschland aufgenommen wurde. „Bearbeitungsklappe [Editing Flap]", der Titel dieses Werks, stellt den Bezug zum Briefeinwurfschlitz her dadurch diesen der der Bearbeitungsvorgang insofern beginnt, als er den Rahmen, der dem Blickwinkel der Kamera gesetzt sind, einschränkt. In diesem durch die Zeit und den Briefeinwurfschlitz geschaffenem Rahmen fanden 24 „Ereignisse" statt, so kehren beispielsweise Menschen vom Einkaufen nach Hause zurück, Autos bringen ihre Besitzer

developed during the making of the drawings.

As well as exploring transdiciplinary editing practices, the book is very much a celebration of the everyday in a very small part of Niederbrechen, Germany. To be honest, mundane events have always rather baffled me. I have no problem considering complex ideas, for example editing and transdisciplinarity, and yet when I am immersed in my work, I can't seem to perform basic everyday tasks such as going shopping for food or cleaning the house. For this reason, I can examine routine from a point of wonder, because it is something that has largely eluded me. So, when considering events such as a woman with a shopping bag, a light being switched on, or a small black cat walking up the road, I found them to be extraordinary examples of beauty and intrigue, and they also raised philosophical and political questions.

The philosophical questions raised during this process relate to ideas around repetition and change. The editing process applied to these events has affected the fundamental nature of what they are, permanently altering them so that they are no longer mundane. Repetition surfaces as a key point within this process, but Jacques Derrida's term 'iteration' is more appropriate. He uses the term

zur Arbeit, und eine Katze dreht wie gewöhnlich ihre Runden. Die Zeichnungen dieses Werks zeigen bearbeitete Versionen dieser 24 Ereignisse, wobei jedes von ihnen zwischen zwei und fünf Zeichnungen umfasst. In einigen Fällen führen die vielfältigen Bearbeitungsvorgänge die Darstellung sehr weit von der ursprünglichen Videoaufnahme weg. Die abschließende Phase des Bearbeitungsvorgangs ist die der Publikation, in der die Zeichnungen zusammengebracht und aneinandergereiht werden. Dies geschieht nicht in chronologischer Reihenfolge, sondern so in einer narrativen Inszenierung, die jene beim Zeichnen entstandenen Ideen widerspiegelt.

So untersucht dieses Buch transdisziplinäre Bearbeitungspraktiken, würdigt jedoch gleichzeitig ganz besonders das alltägliche Leben in einem sehr kleinen Teil von Niederbrechen in Deutschland. Alltägliche Ereignisse haben mich, ehrlich gesagt schon immer ziemlich erstaunt. Es fällt mir nicht schwer, mich mit komplexen Themen wie beispielsweise Bearbeitungsprozessen und Transdisziplinarität auseinanderzusetzen, und doch kann ich mich, wenn ich in meine Arbeit vertieft bin, nicht mit den Dingen des täglichen Lebens wie zum Beispiel

in his 1972 essay 'Signature Event Context', and it does not simply signify repetition as in 'reiteration', but every iteration is an alteration, or a modification. Derrida suggests that iteration makes communicative utterances become living and endless, infinite in their iterability (1982, p. 316). He explains that because of its essential iterability, a written sign can always be detached from its context without causing it to lose all possibility of functioning as communication. 'No context can enclose it' (Derrida, 1982, p. 317). Although Derrida discusses communicative expression in terms of writing, I am taking into account all communicative fields, including editing video and drawing. In this publication, I use iteration to see if the events can survive the stripping away of their original context and can function in a new way, as an examination of editing processes, which are also infinitely repeatable.

Political ideas brought up by the process of making this publication relate to how real life is edited, and ideas around agency within that process – something I began looking at in my last book *[Video] Klappe* (2014). I also had to consider issues around privacy relating to recording in public spaces. To explain this last point, the events in this book take place in the space outside my

einkaufen gehen oder das Haus putzen, befassen. Aus diesem Grund gelingt es mir, Routine aus einer Perspektive des Staunens zu betrachten, da diese mich weitgehend verschont hat. Als ich mich also mit Ereignissen wie einer Frau, die vom Einkaufen kommt, mit, dem Einschalten des Lichts oder einer kleinen schwarzen Katze, die die Straße entlangläuft, auseinandersetzte, empfand ich diese als außergewöhnliche Beispiele von Schönheit und Faszination, die zugleich auch politische und philosophische Fragen aufwarfen.

Die philosophischen Fragen, die hier aufkamen, drehen sich um Ideen von Wiederholung und Veränderung. Der Bearbeitungsprozess, dem diese Ereignisse unterzogen wurden, hat sin ihrer grundlegenden Natur beeinflusst und sie dauerhaft verändert, so dass sie nicht länger alltäglich sind. Wiederholung erscheint als ein Schlüsselbegriff dieses Vorgangs, aber besser trifft es Jacques Derridas „Iteration". Er verwendet diesen Begriff in seinem Werk „Signature Event Context" von 1972. Wiederholung ist für ihn nicht einfach etwas, was sich noch einmal ereignet, vielmehr ist jede Iteration ein Wandel oder eine Modifizierung. Derrida sagt, dass Iteration kommunikative Äußerungen zum Leben erweckt und unendlich werden lässt, unendlich

house, which is public and not part of my property. A short time after I had completed the filming, I found out that making the recording through my letterbox was actually illegal in Germany. Oh dear. My actions were never motivated by any malicious intention to record people covertly, and at the point of doing it I was not aware that I was breaking the law. Had I known about the law, then I would have put a sign up on my front door to inform people that filming was taking place (even though that would have resulted in the video depicting curious neighbours climbing up my front steps to read the sign...). However, rather than abandon the entire project, I decided that I could go ahead and use the edited video material as long as the original footage wasn't included in the final images and my drawings did not identify any specific people. Under these self-imposed rules, I felt that I could continue with my editing process and move forward towards publication. As it turned out, this restriction was an interesting challenge and allowed me the freedom to just draw and to see where the editing process would take me.

Drawing has always been my primary method for thinking through conceptual, philosophical and political ideas. One of the reasons for this is that it is such an inclusive medium:

in ihrer Iterabilität (1982, Seite 316). Er erklärt, dass auf Grund seiner essentiellen Iterabilität ein Schriftzeichen immer seinem Kontext entnommen werden kann, ohne dass es dabei die Möglichkeit, als Kommunikation zu funktionieren, verliert. „Kein Kontext kann es einschließen" (Derrida, 1982, Seite 317). Obwohl Derrida kommunikativen Ausdruck ausschließlich in Bezug auf das Schreiben diskutiert, ziehe ich alle Kommunikationsfelder mit ein, einschließlich jener der Videobearbeitung und der Zeichnung. In diesem Werk verwende ich Iteration um zu sehen, ob die Ereignisse das Herauslösen aus ihrem ursprünglichen Kontext überstehen und auf neue Art und Weise funktionieren können. - in einer Untersuchung der Bearbeitungsprozesse, die auch unendlich wiederholbar sind.

Die politischen Gedanken, die bei der Erstellung dieses Werkes aufkamen, beziehen sich auf die Art und Weise der Bearbeitung des realen und Vorstellung der Wirkung innerhalb dieses Prozesses - etwas, das ich in meinem letzten Buch *[Video] Klappe* (2014) zu untersuchen begann. Bei den Aufnahmen im öffentlichen Raum musste ich auch Bestimmungen zur Privatsphäre beachten. Genau gesagt, finden die in diesem Buch gezeigten Ereignisse außerhalb

'What's at drawing's centre? No one thing, for certain. Its inclusivity is too great for that to be true – what cannot be represented by drawing? But its inexhaustible capacity for invention and change [...] has a lot to do with this inclusivity, with the range of content that it can deal with, and not so much to do with material experimentation.' (Ginsborg, 2003, p. 11)

If drawing is a medium of inclusivity, already used in such a broad number of disciplines and for so many different purposes, for example in architecture, engineering or linguistics as well as fine art, then using it in video editing is a natural progression – and it provided me with a strategy for thinking through the editing process in a new way. The concept of drawing being 'language at full stretch' (Maynard, 2005, p.4) is appropriate to the way that I use drawing for editing video, and it has become an effective strategy for testing the representational and expressive limits of experimental video. Drawing enhances the technical function of editing in two ways. Firstly, it provides a new way for manipulating the video material, even allowing for the removal of the original footage, as in this book. Secondly, because drawing 'renders thought visible' (Petherbridge, 2010, p. 2) it serves a clear purpose in making editing processes visible.

Drawing is part of my transdisciplinary

meines Hauses, also im öffentlichen Raum und nicht auf meinem Grundstück statt. Kurz nachdem ich alles gefilmt hatte, fand ich heraus, dass dies in Deutschland eigentlich nicht erlaubt ist. Oje! Mein Handeln ist niemals durch irgendeine böse Absicht, Menschen ohne ihr Wissen zu filmen, motiviert gewesen. Als ich dies tat, war mir nicht bewusst, dass ich rechtlichen Bestimmungen zuwiderhandelte. Wäre mir die Rechtslage bekannt gewesen wäre, hätte ich ein Hinweisschild an meiner Haustüre angebracht, um die Menschen zu informieren, dass hier gefilmt wird. (Selbst wenn dies dazu geführt hätte, dass das Video neugierige Nachbarn gezeigt hätte, die die Stufen zu meiner Eingangstüre hochgekommen wären, um das Schild zu lesen....). Statt aber das ganze Projekt aufzugeben, entschied ich, weiterzumachen und verwendete das bearbeitete Videomaterial soweit, dass die ursprünglichen Aufnahmen nicht in den endgültigen Darstellungen zu finden waren und meine Zeichnungen keine identifizierbaren Menschen zeigten. Diesen selbstgewählten Regeln folgend, konnte ich guten Gewissens mit dem Editieren fortfahren und zur Veröffentlichung schreiten. Wie sich herausstellte, war diese Einschränkung eine interessante Herausforderung und sie gab mir die Freiheit, einfach zu zeichnen und zu sehen, wohin der Bearbeitungsprozess mich führen

approach for editing video. It is a unified approach that differs from disciplinary research because it 'concerns the dynamics engendered by the action of several levels of Reality at once' (Nicolescu, 2008, p. 3), where research within one discipline deals with just one level of Reality at a time. Nicolescu explains that Reality, with a capital 'R', designates 'that which resists our experiences, representations, descriptions, images, or even mathematical formulations' (2008. p. 4), that Reality is 'connected to resistance in our human experience' (2008. p. 4). While transdisciplinarity is concerned with coherence and unity, it is also formed from a position of resistance, and this is appropriate for my practice, which has consistently resisted being categorised. The 'Charter of Transdisciplinarity' states that 'the keystone of transdisciplinarity is the semantic and practical unification of the meanings that traverse and lay beyond different disciplines' and that it is *resolutely open*' (Nicolescu, 2008, p. 263). This 'open' position, resisting specific categorisation, is the most authentic position from which to view my practice.

würde.

Zeichnen ist für mich seit jeher die vorrangige Methode, konzeptionelle, philosophische und politische Gedanken zu verarbeiten. Einer der Gründe hierfür ist, dass diese Medium so Vieles mit einschließt.

„Was steht im Mittelpunkt des Zeichnens? Sicherlich nicht eine Sache. Seine Inklusivität ist zu groß, als dass das wahr sein könnte - was kann durch Zeichnen nicht dargestellt werden? Aber seine unerschöpfliche Fähigkeit zur Erfindung und Veränderung [.....] hat viel mit dieser Inklusivität zu tun, mit der Bandbreite des Inhaltes, mit dem es sich auseinandersetzen kann, und nicht so viel mit materiellem Experimentieren." (Ginsborg, 2003, Seite 11)

Wenn Zeichnen ein Medium der Inklusivität ist, das bereits in vielen Bereichen und für so viele unterschiedliche Zwecke genutzt wird , sei es beispielsweise in der Architektur, im Ingenieurswesen, in der Linguistik oder auch in der Kunst, dann ist der Einsatz des Zeichnens in der Videobearbeitung ein natürlicher nächster Schritt - und mir bot es eine Strategie, Prozess des Editierens auf neue Art und Weise zu betrachten. Das Konzept des Zeichnens als einer „Sprache mit voller Kraft" eignet sich für die Art, in der ich Zeichnen zur Videobearbeitung einsetze. Es wurde zu einer effektiven Strategie,

References:

Derrida, J. (1982) 'Signature Event Context'. In *Margins of Philosophy*. Translated by Alan Bass. Chicago: The University of Chicago Press. Originally published in 1972.

Ginsborg, M. (2003) 'Preface: What is Drawing?'. In: Kingston, A. *What is Drawing?* London: Black Dog Publishing.

Maynard, P. (2005) *Drawing Distinctions: The Varieties of Graphic Expression*. Ithaca, NY: Cornell University Press.

Nicolescu, B. (2008) *Transdisciplinarity: Theory and Practice*. Cresskill: Hampton Press.

Petherbridge, D. (2010) *The Primacy of Drawing*. New Haven/London: Yale University Press.

Rees, A. L. (1999) *A History of Experimental Film and Video*. London: British Film Institute.

die Grenzen der Darstellung und des Ausdrucks des experimentellen Videos zu testen. Zeichnen bringt die technische Funktion der Bearbeitung in zweierlei Hinsicht voran. Erstens bietet es eine neue Möglichkeit, das Videomaterial zu verändern, die es sogar erlaubt, wie in diesem Buch das ursprüngliche Filmmaterial zu entfernen. Zweitens dient das Zeichnen, da es „Gedanken sichtbar macht" (Petherbridge, 2010, Seite 2), klar dem Zweck, Bearbeitungsvorgänge sichtbar zu machen.

Zeichnen ist Teil meines transdisziplinären Ansatzes der Videobearbeitung. Es ist ein einheitlicher Ansatz, der sich von der disziplinären Forschung abhebt, da er „ die Dynamik betrifft, die von der gleichzeitigen Aktion verschiedener Ebenen der Realität geschaffen wird" (Nicolescu, 2008, Seite 3). Forschung innerhalb einer Disziplin beschäftigt sich nur mit jeweils einer Realitätsebene. Nicolescu legt dar, dass der Begriff Realität, der sich in diesem Zusammenhang auch im Englischen mit einem großem „R" schreibt, das bezeichnet, „was sich unseren Erfahrungen, Darstellungen, Beschreibungen, Vorstellungen oder sogar mathematischen Formulierungen widersetzt" (2008, Seite 4), dass Realität in diesem Sinne „in Verbindung mit Widerstand in unserer menschlichen

Erfahrung steht" (2008, Seite 4). Während es bei Transdisziplininarität um Kohärenz und Einheit geht, bildet sie sich auch aus einer Position des Widerstandes. Dies passt zu meiner Vorgehensweise, die sich stets dem Kategorisieren widersetzt hat. Die „Charta der Transdisziplinarität" legt dar, „dass der Grundpfeiler der Transdisziplinarität die semantische und praktische Vereinigung der Bedeutungen ist, die verschiedene Disziplinen durchziehen und über sie hinausgehen" und dass sie „resolut offen" ist (Nicolescu, 2008, Seite 263). Diese *„offene Position"*, die sich deutlicher Kategorisierung widersetzt, ist die authentischste Position, aus der meine Vorgehensweise zu betrachten ist.

Referenzen:

Derrida, J. (1982) „Signature Event Context". In *Margins of Philosophy*. Übersetzt von Alan Bass. Chicago: The University of Chicago Press. Zuerst veröffentlicht 1972.

Ginsborg, M. (2003) 'Preface: What is Drawing?'. In: Kingston, A. *What is Drawing?* London: Black Dog Publishing.

Maynard, P. (2005) *Drawing Distinctions: The Varieties of Graphic Expression*. Ithaca, NY: Cornell University Press.

16

Nicolescu, B. (2008) *Transdisciplinarity: Theory and Practice.* Cresskill: Hampton Press.

Petherbridge, D. (2010) *The Primacy of Drawing.* New Haven/London: Yale University Press.

Rees, A. L. (1999) *A History of Experimental Film and Video.* London: British Film Institute.

drawings
Zeichnungen

RED BUCKET MAN/MANN MIT ROTEM EIMER

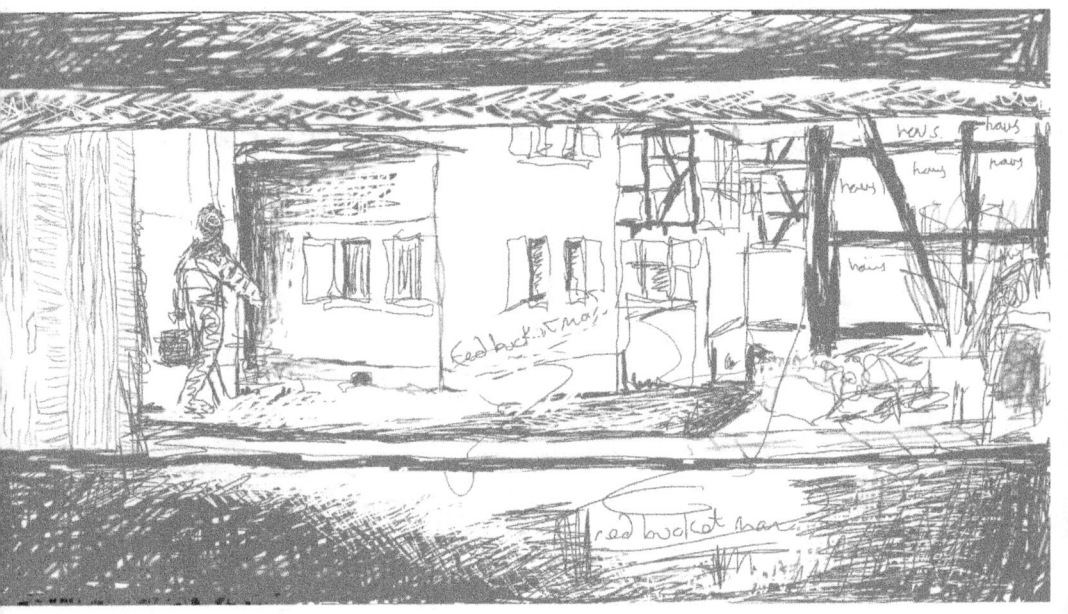

RED BUCKET MAN/MANN MIT ROTEM EIMER

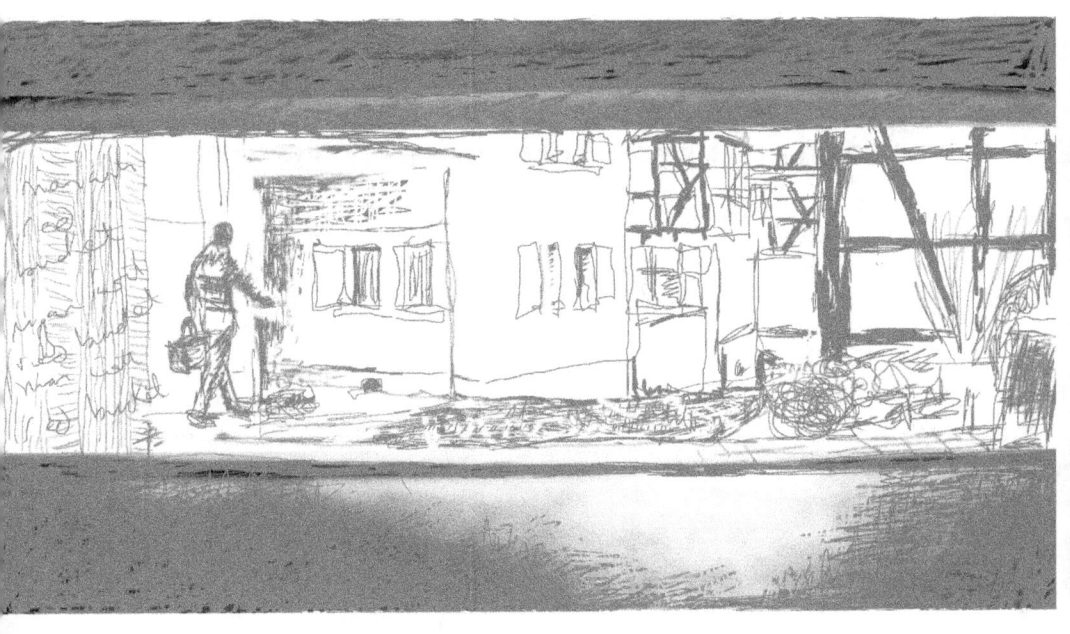

RED BUCKET MAN/MANN MIT ROTEM EIMER

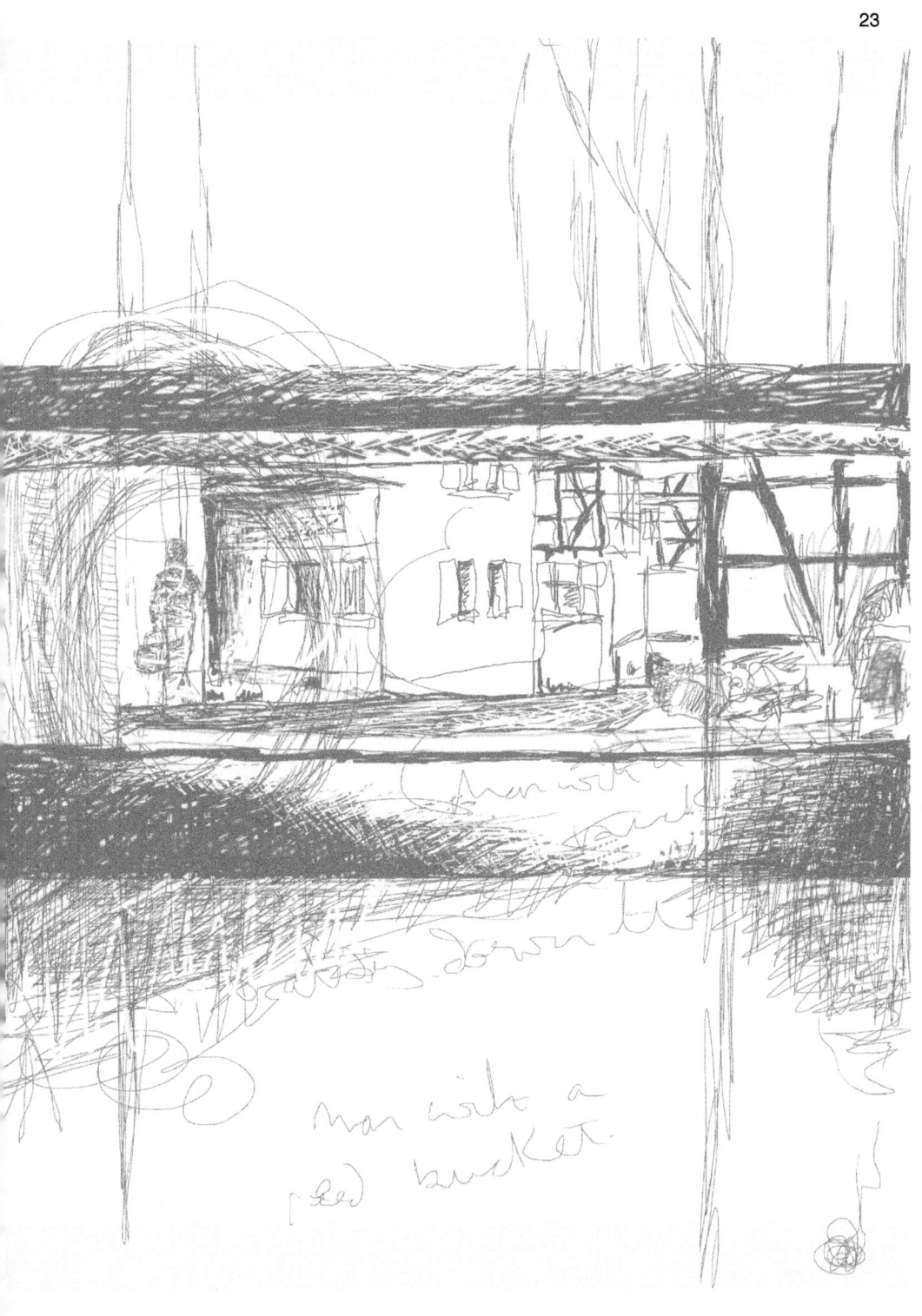

man with a
reed bucket.

RED BUCKET MAN/MANN MIT ROTEM EIMER

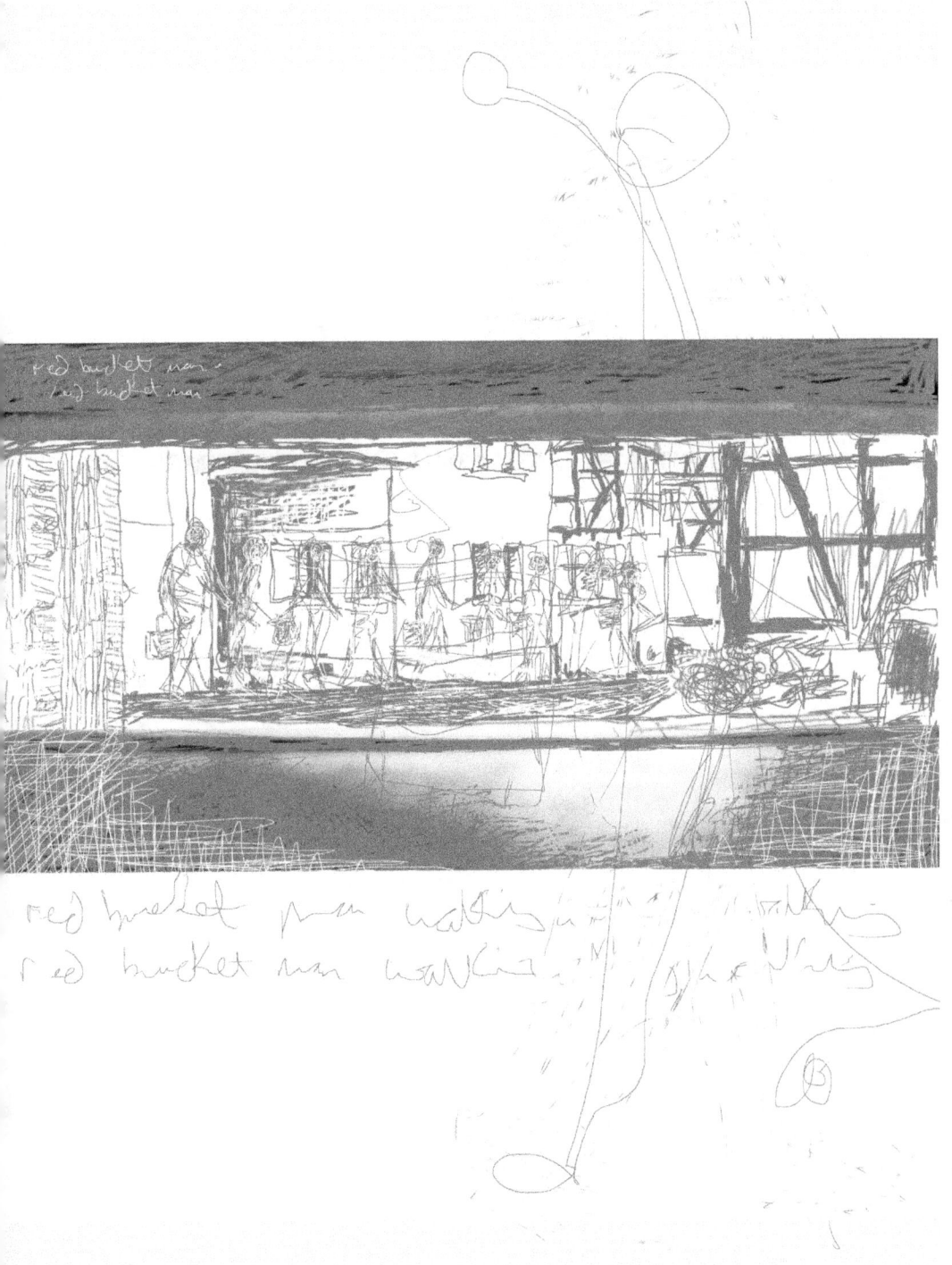

red bucket man-
red bucket man

red bucket man walking
red bucket man walking

RED BUCKET MAN/MANN MIT ROTEM EIMER

still the man with the red bucket.
its actually a shopping
basket and not a bucket at all.

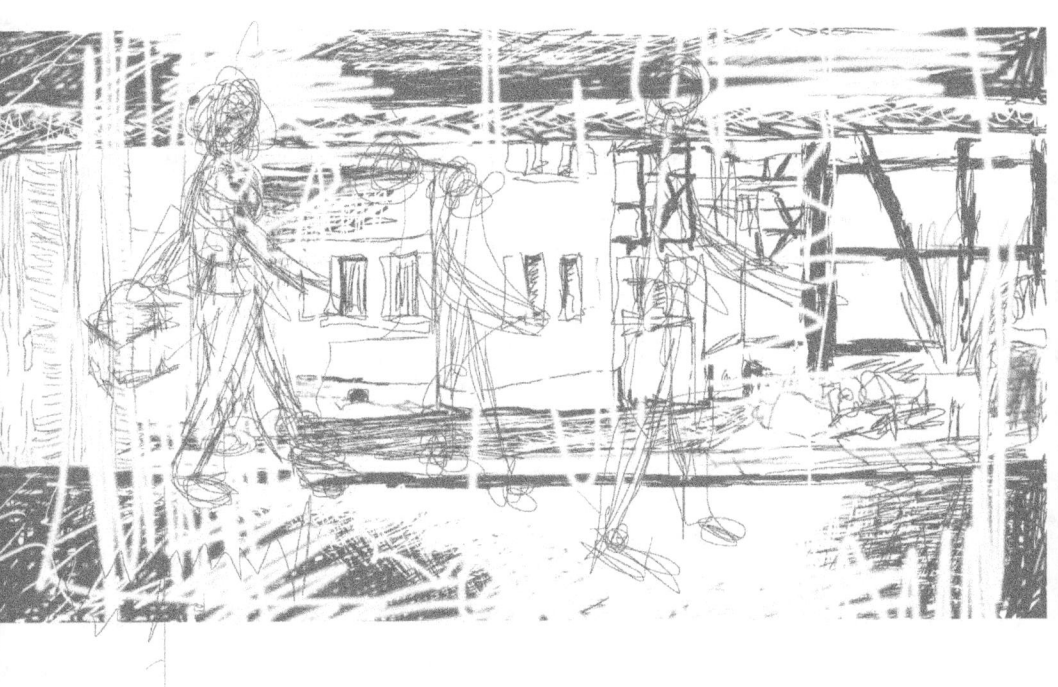

blind drawing regarding of
n reference to the original
material.

MERCEDES APPROACHING/MERCEDES KOMMT NÄHER.

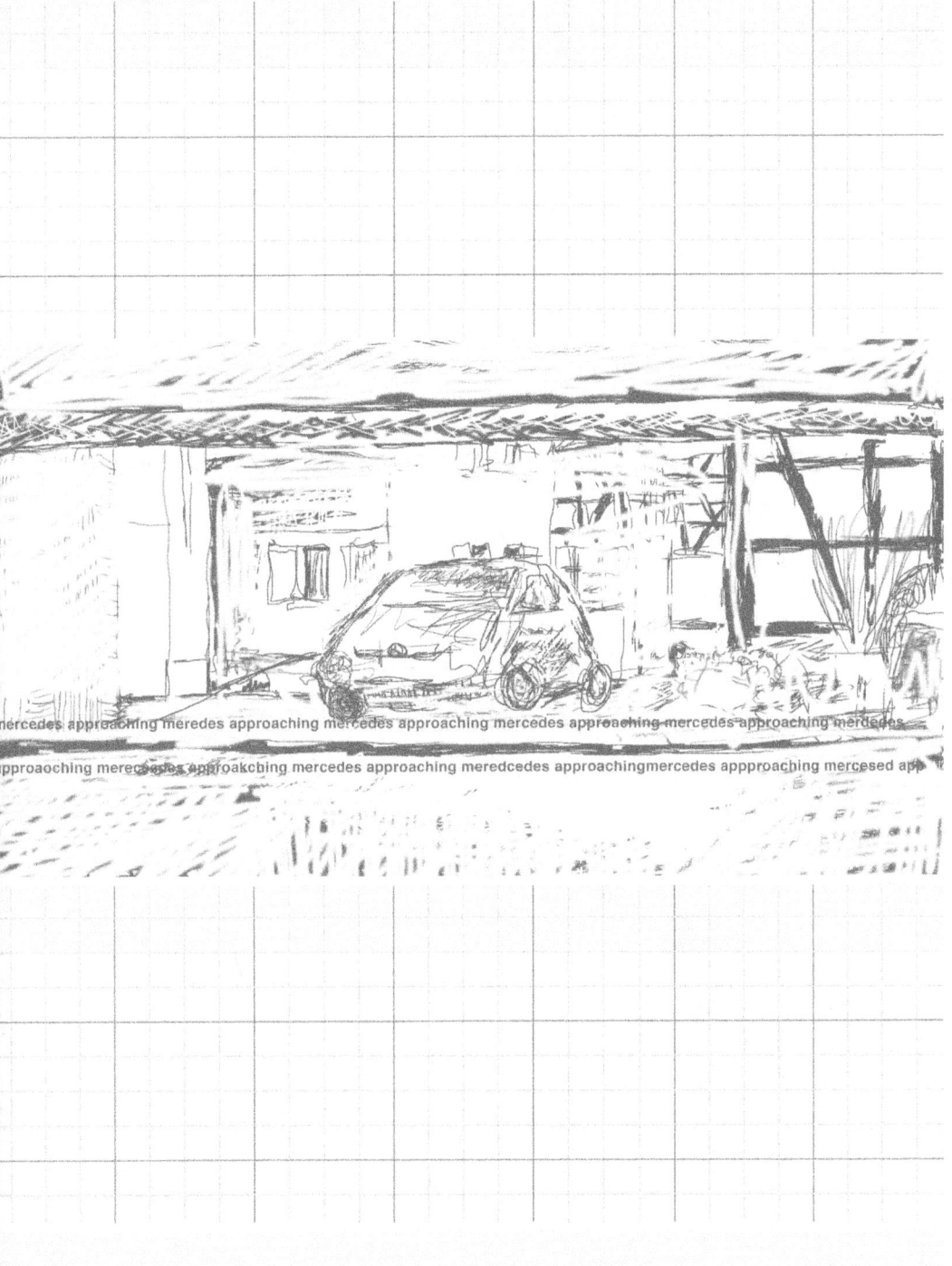

mercedes approaching meredes approaching mercedes approaching mercedes approaching mercedes approaching merdedes

approaoching mercesedes approakching mercedes approaching meredcedes approachingmercedes appproaching mercesed app

MERCEDES APPROACHING/MERCEDES KOMMT NÄHER

I know someone who drives a mercedes. re-edit
I know someone who drives a mercedes. re-edit
I know someone who drives a mercedes. re-edit
I know a man who drives a mercedes. re-edit
I know a man who drives a mercedes. re-edit
I know someone who drives a mercedes. re-edit
I know a man who drives a mercedes. re-edit
I know a man who drives a mercedes. re-edit
I know a man who drives a re-edit
I know a man who drives a re-edit
I know a man who drives a re-edit
I know a man who drives a mercedes. re-edit
I know someone who drives a mercedes. re-edit
I know a man who drives a mercedes. re-edit

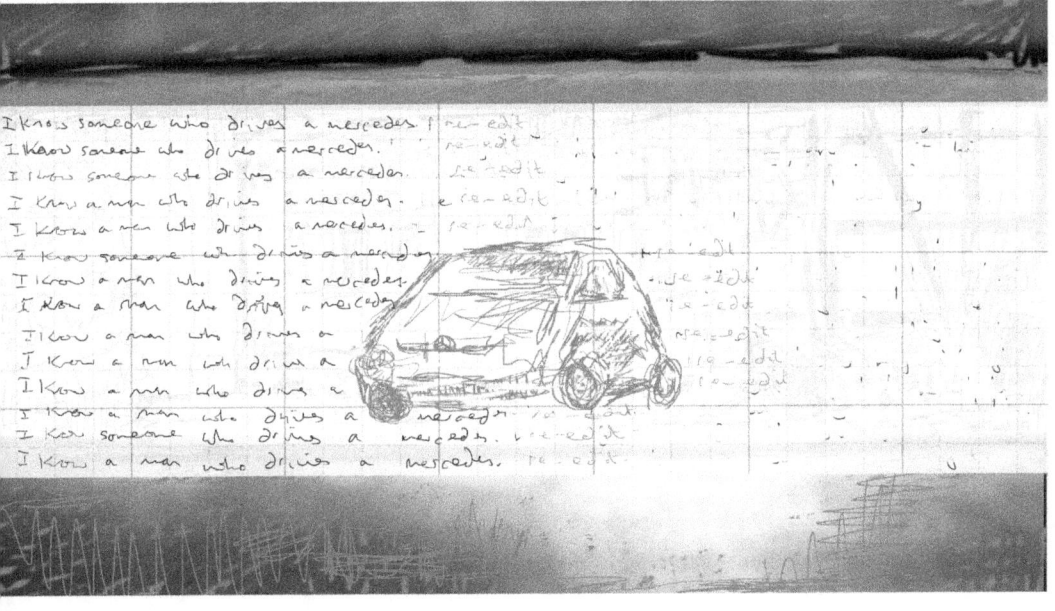

MERCEDES APPROACHING/MERCEDES KOMMT NÄHER

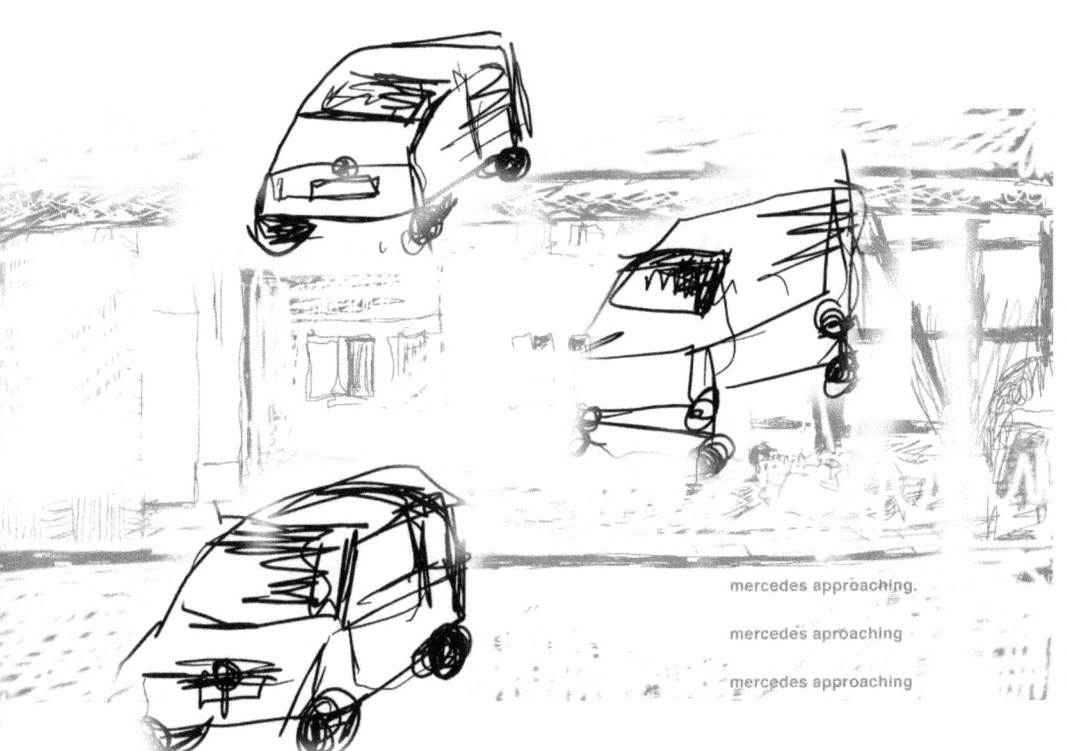

mercedes approaching.

mercedes aproaching

mercedes approaching

PERSON IN RED COAT/MENSCH IM ROTEN MANTEL

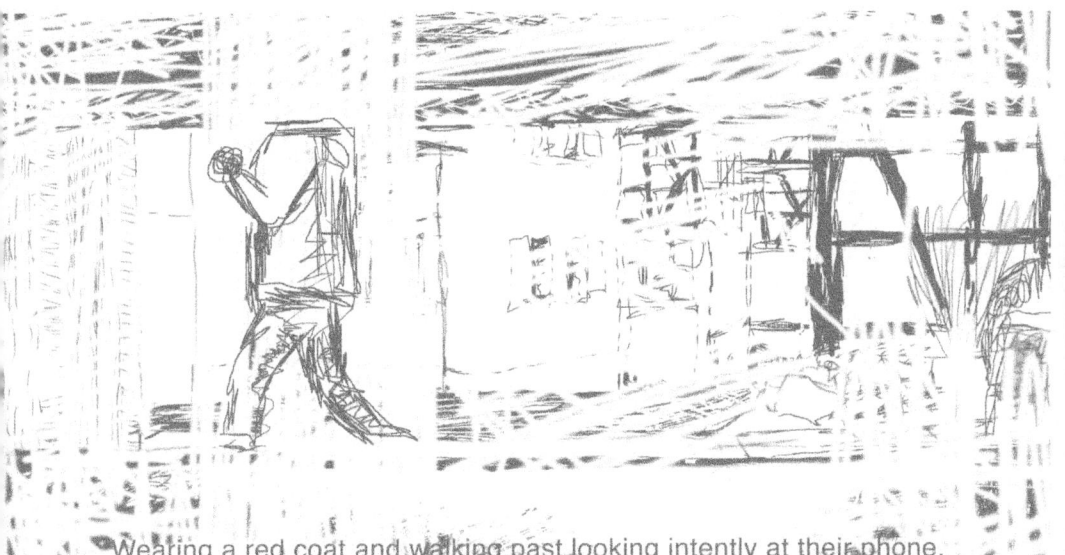

Wearing a red coat and walking past looking intently at their phone.
Wearing a red coat and walking past looking intently at their phone.
Wearing a red coat and walking past looking intently at their phone.
Wearing a red coat and walking past looking intently at their phone.

PERSON IN RED COAT/MENSCH IM ROTEN MANTEL

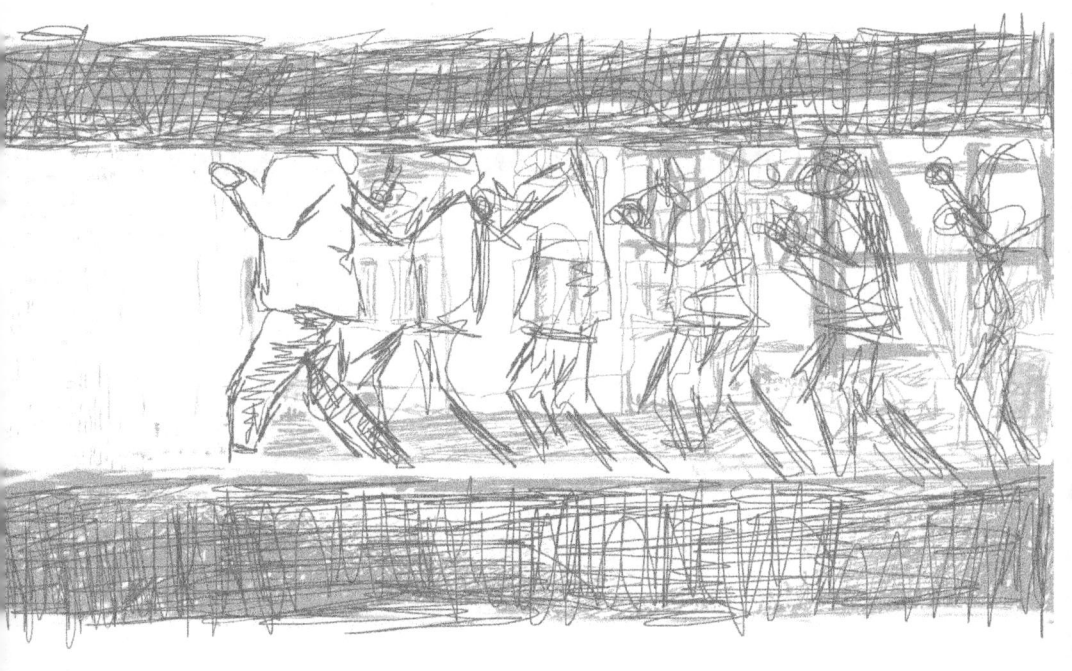

PERSON IN RED COAT/MENSCH IM ROTEN MANTEL

and we don't know what is happening
outside of the frame. her legs might be
eight metres long and her head might
extend into a cone shape. and we
don't know where she has come from,
or what is so interesting on her phone.

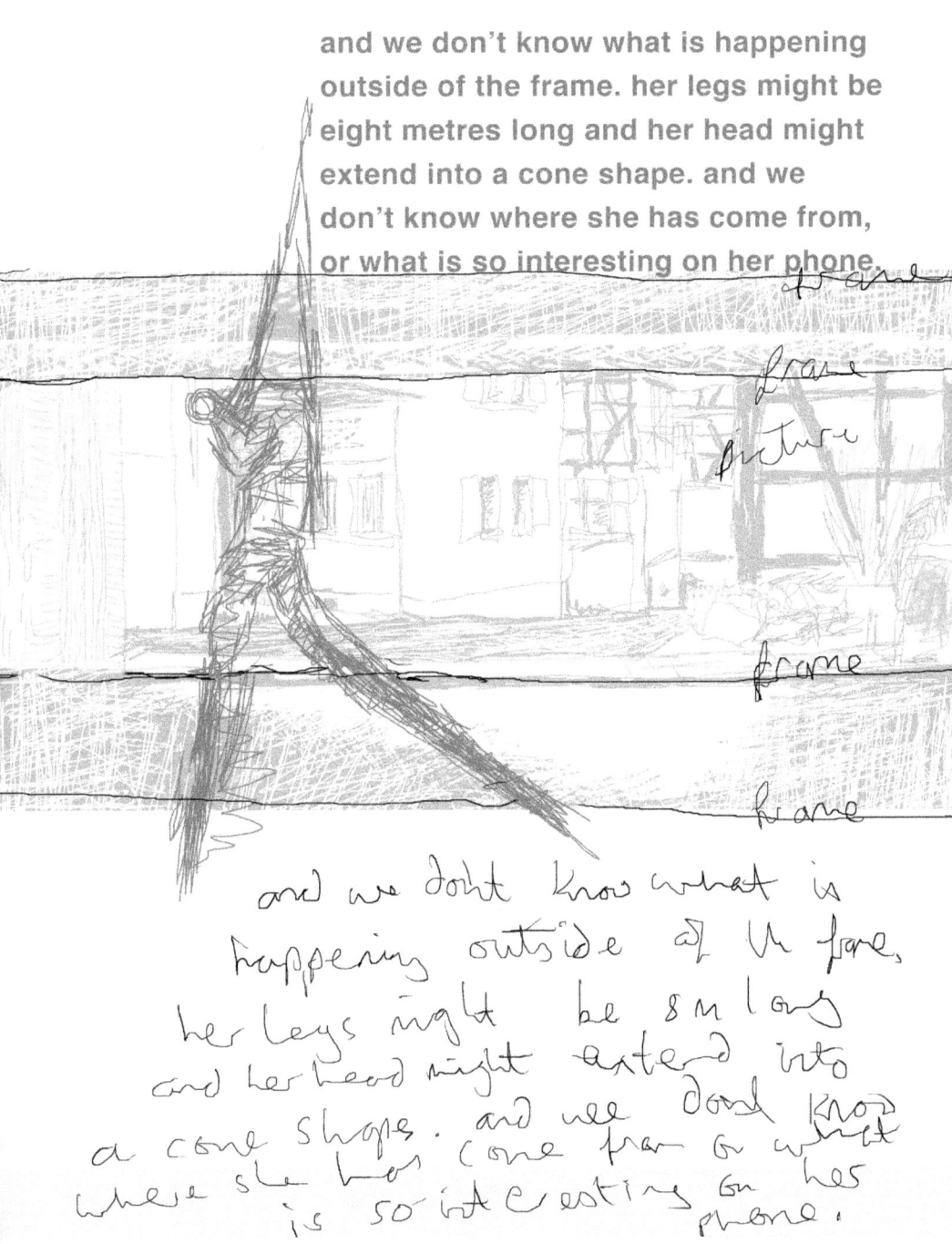

frame
frame
picture
frame
frame

and we don't know what is
happening outside of the frame.
her legs might be 8m long
and her head might extend into
a cone shape. and we don't know
where she has come from or what
is so interesting on her
phone.

LIGHT ON/LICHT AN

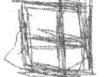

Light on

LIGHT ON/LICHT AN

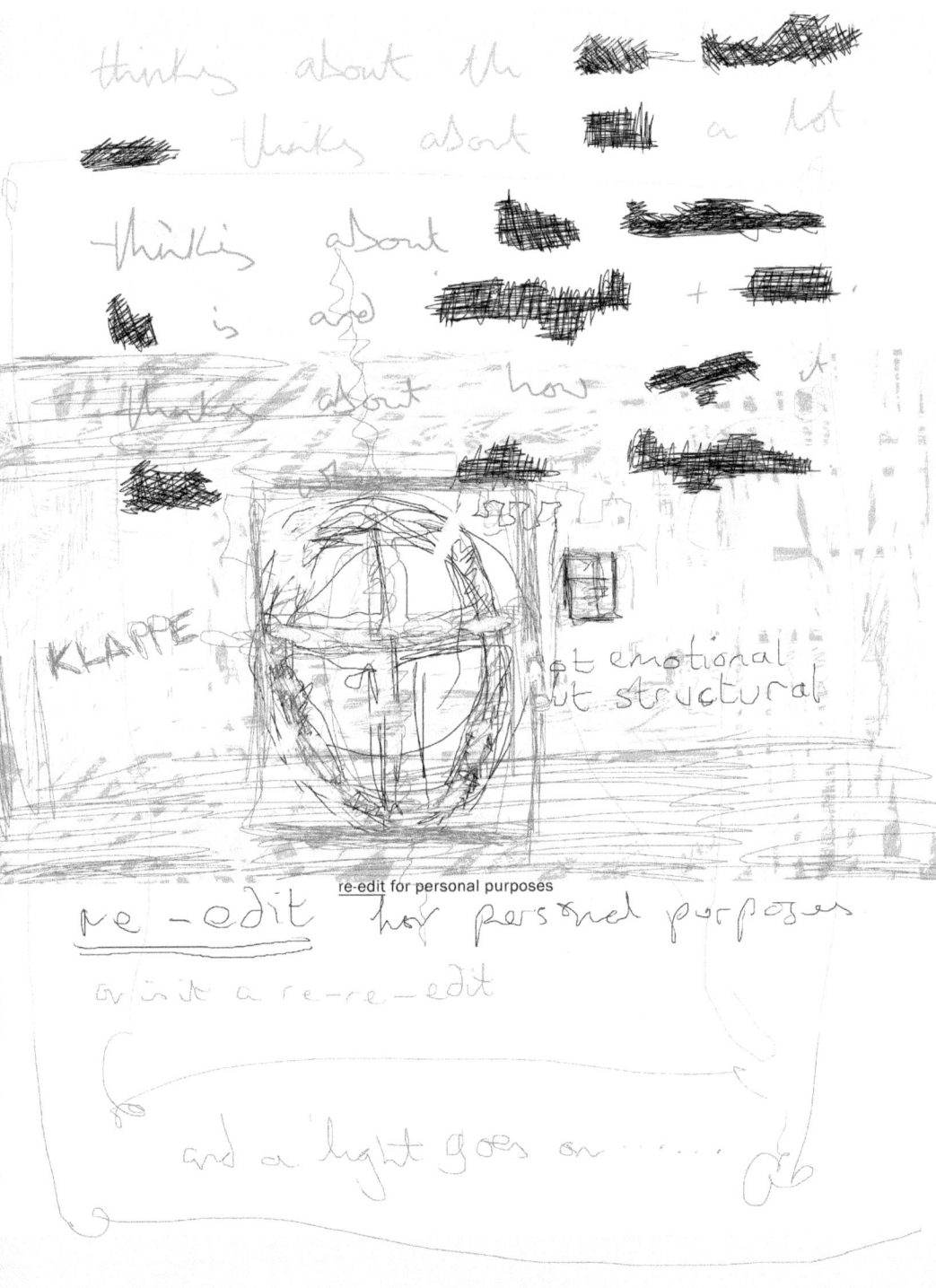

thinking about th

thinking about a lot

thinking about

is and

thinking about how

KLAPPE

ot emotional
ut structural

re-edit for personal purposes

re - edit for personal purposes

or is it a re-re-edit

and a light goes on . . . . . .

LIGHT ON/LICHT AN

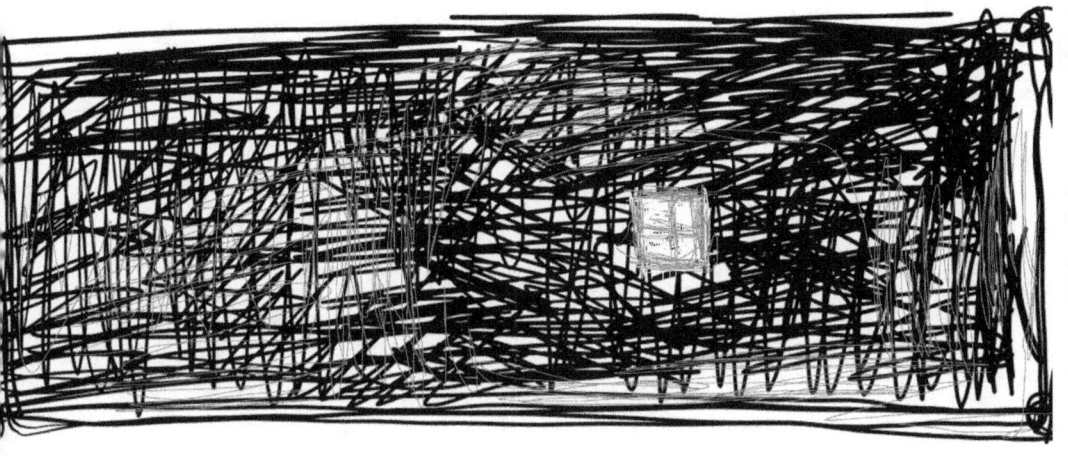

Light on

light on

light on

light on

LIGHT ON/LICHT AN

light on   light on

light on

light on

light on

light on

SMALL BLACK CAT/KLEINE SCHWARZE KATZE

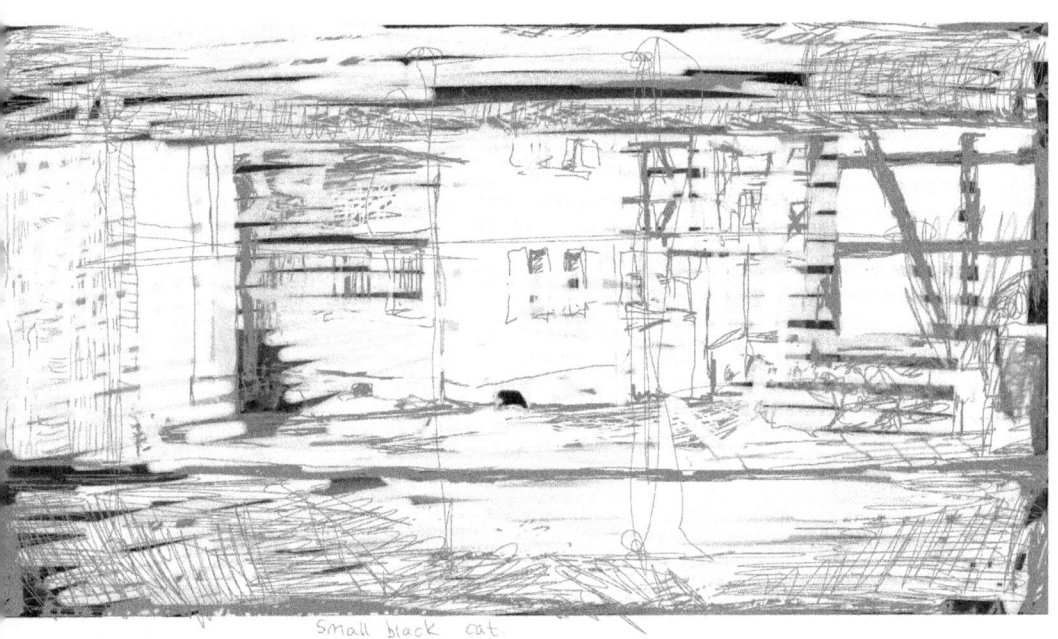

Small black cat.

SMALL BLACK CAT/KLEINE SCHWARZE KATZE

Pixie wasn't small or black. She was tortoiseshell and very heavy, in fact she weighed nearly a stone. Half of her face was black and half of her face was ginger, under her chin she had a white bib. She was a beautiful cat. She was very special, very intelligent and very understanding of my moods. She never killed anything in her life, not even a bug. She would climb onto me first thing in the morning and last thing at night, every morning and night, and purr into my hair and dribble on me and make kissy noises. She loved me unconditionally. One evening we put up the christmas tree and in the morning I think she had forgotten what we had done, so she 'discovered' the tree in the living room, and immediately woke me up and insisted that I come downstairs with her to see what she had found. The same happened the first time she saw snow outside. A couple of years later, the council called round to do a spot check to check my identity or something. They rang my doorbell very early and got me out of bed. This prevented Pixie from having her routine morning cuddle so she insisted on sitting on my back and purring into my hair while I was trying to talk to the people from the council.

Pixie wasn't small or black. She was tortoiseshell and very heavy, in fact she weighed nearly a stone. Half of her face was black and half of her face was ginger, under her chin she had a white bib. She was a beautiful cat. She was very special, very intelligent and very understanding of my moods. She never killed anything in her life, not even a bug. She would climb onto me first thing in the morning and last thing at night, every morning and night, and purr into my hair and dribble on me and make kissy noises. She loved me unconditionally. One evening we put up the christmas tree and in the morning I think she had forgotten what we had done, so she 'discovered' the tree in the living room, and immediately woke me up and insisted that I come downstairs with her to see what she had found. The same happened the first time she saw snow outside. A couple of years later, the council called round to do a spot check to check my identity or something. They rang my doorbell very early and got me out of bed. This prevented Pixie from having her routine morning cuddle so she insisted on sitting on my back and purring into my hair while I was trying to talk to the people from the council.

TWO PEOPLE/ZWEI MENSCHEN

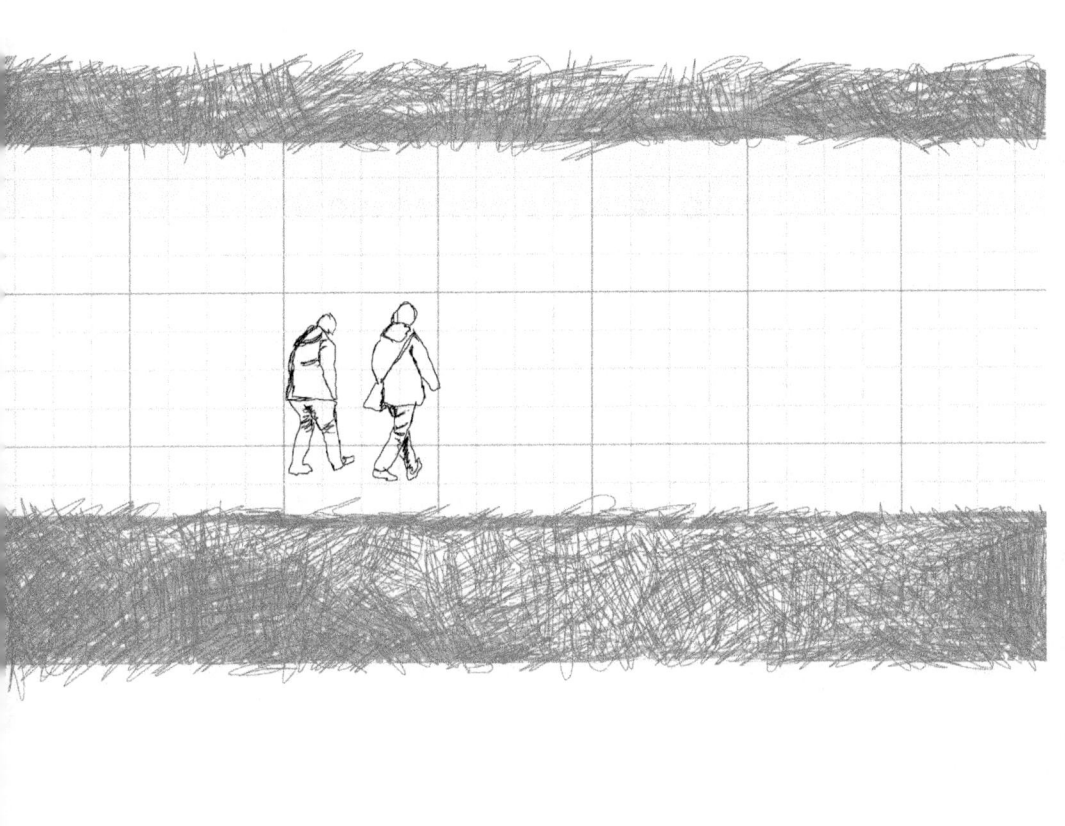

TWO PEOPLE/ZWEI MENSCHEN

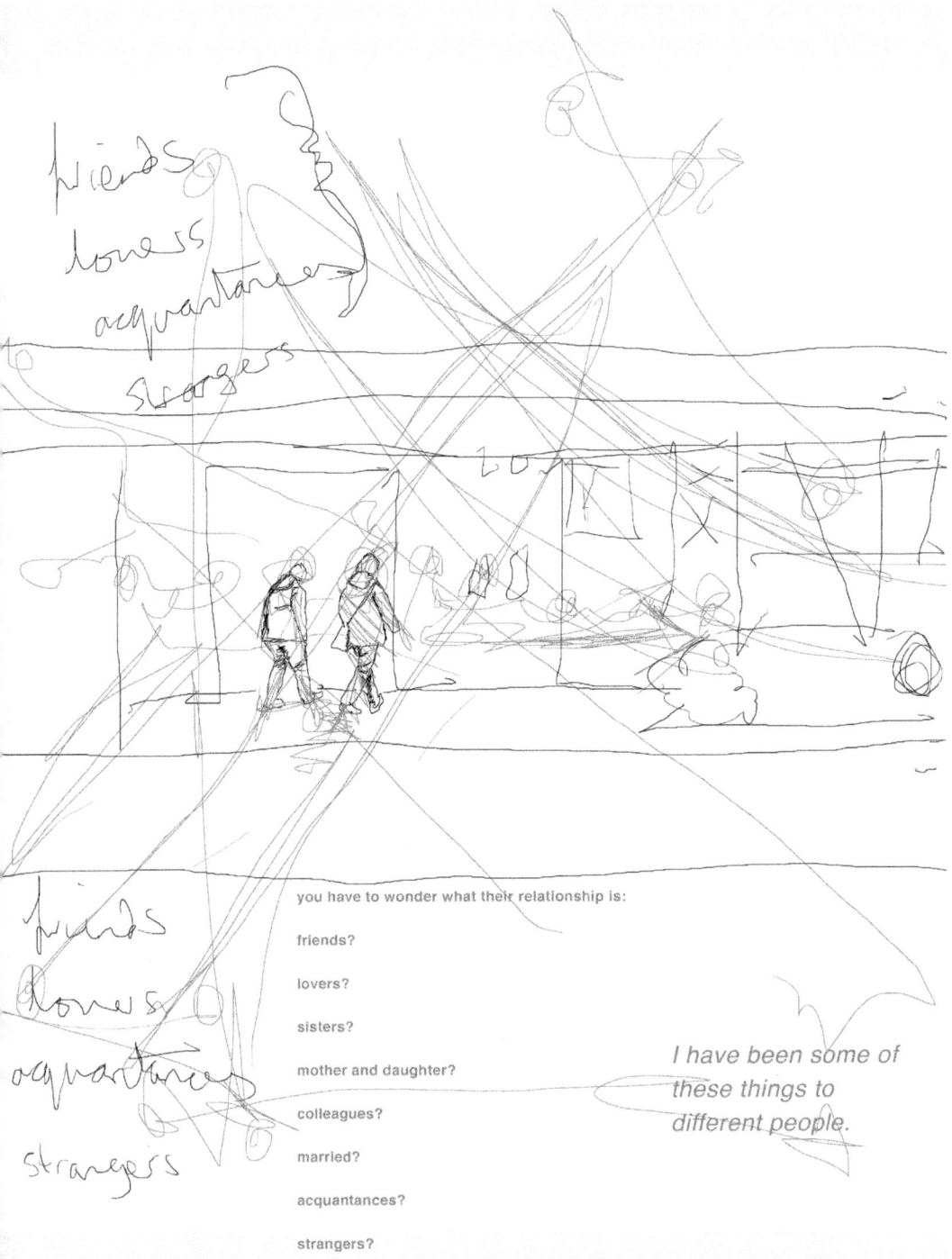

friends
lovers
acquantances
strangers

friends
lovers
acquantances
strangers

you have to wonder what their relationship is:

friends?

lovers?

sisters?

mother and daughter?

colleagues?

married?

acquantances?

strangers?

I have been some of these things to different people.

VAN/WAGEN

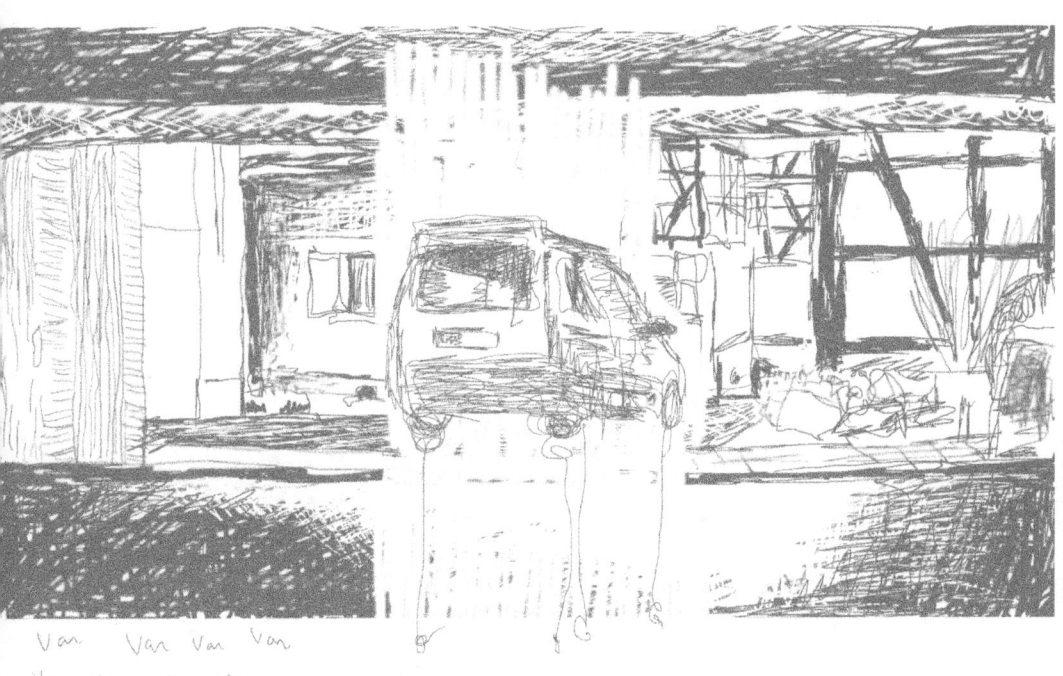

Van Van Van Van
Van Van Van Van
Van Van Van Van
Van Van Van Van
Van Van Van Van
Van Van Van Va

Van Van Van
Van Van
Van Van

a white van with a
window in the back
and a roof rack.
black wheels

VAN/WAGEN

exeins van/lights.
Moving away from the house
down the road.

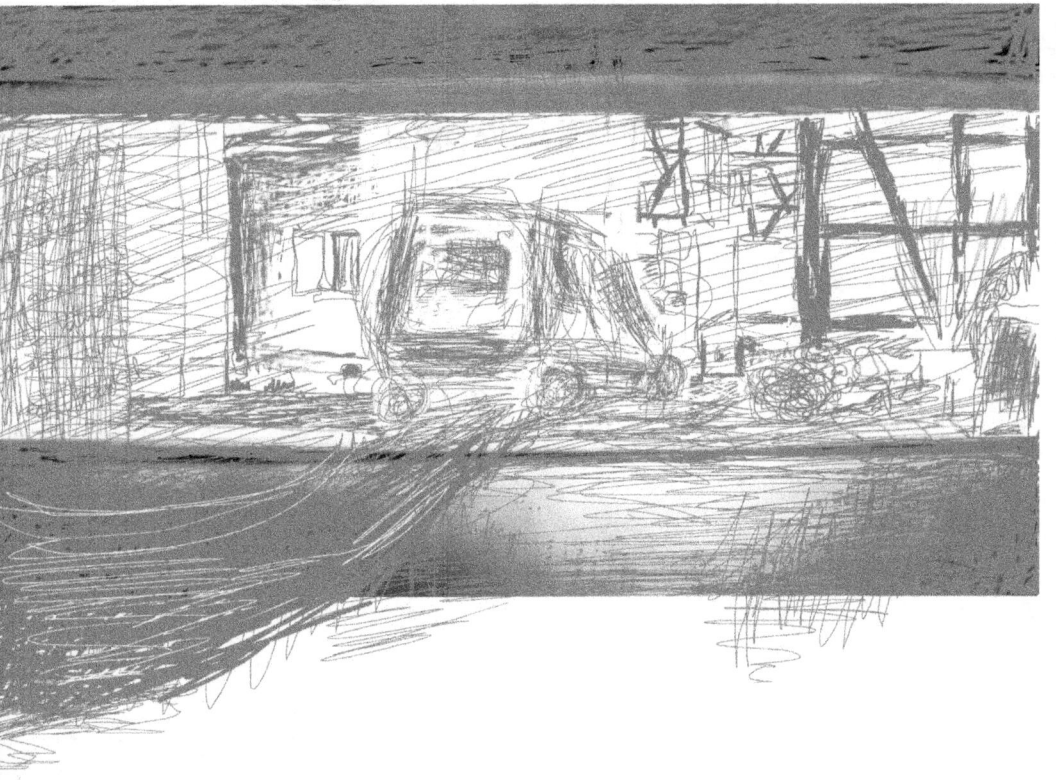

VAN/WAGEN

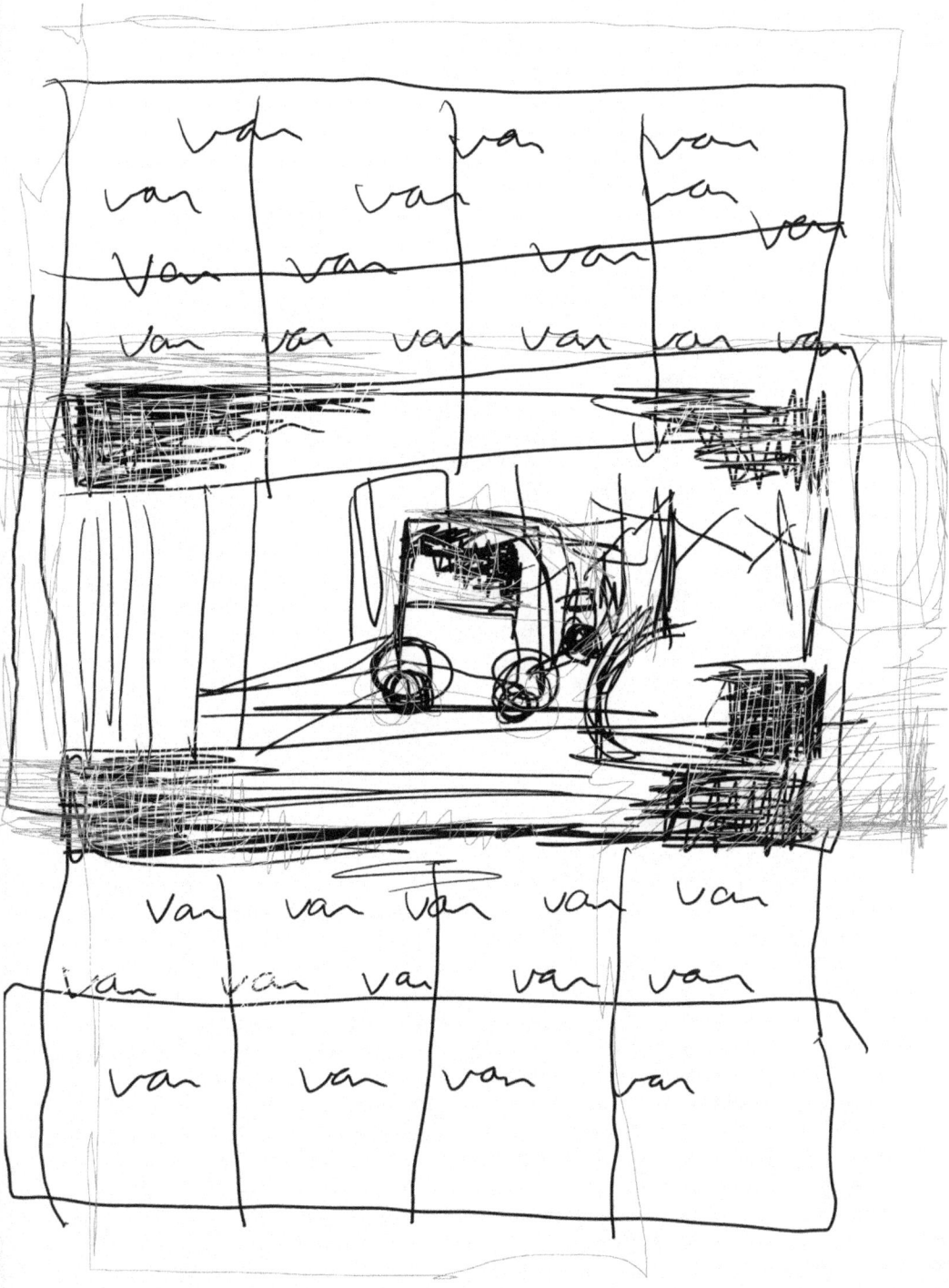

VAN/WAGEN

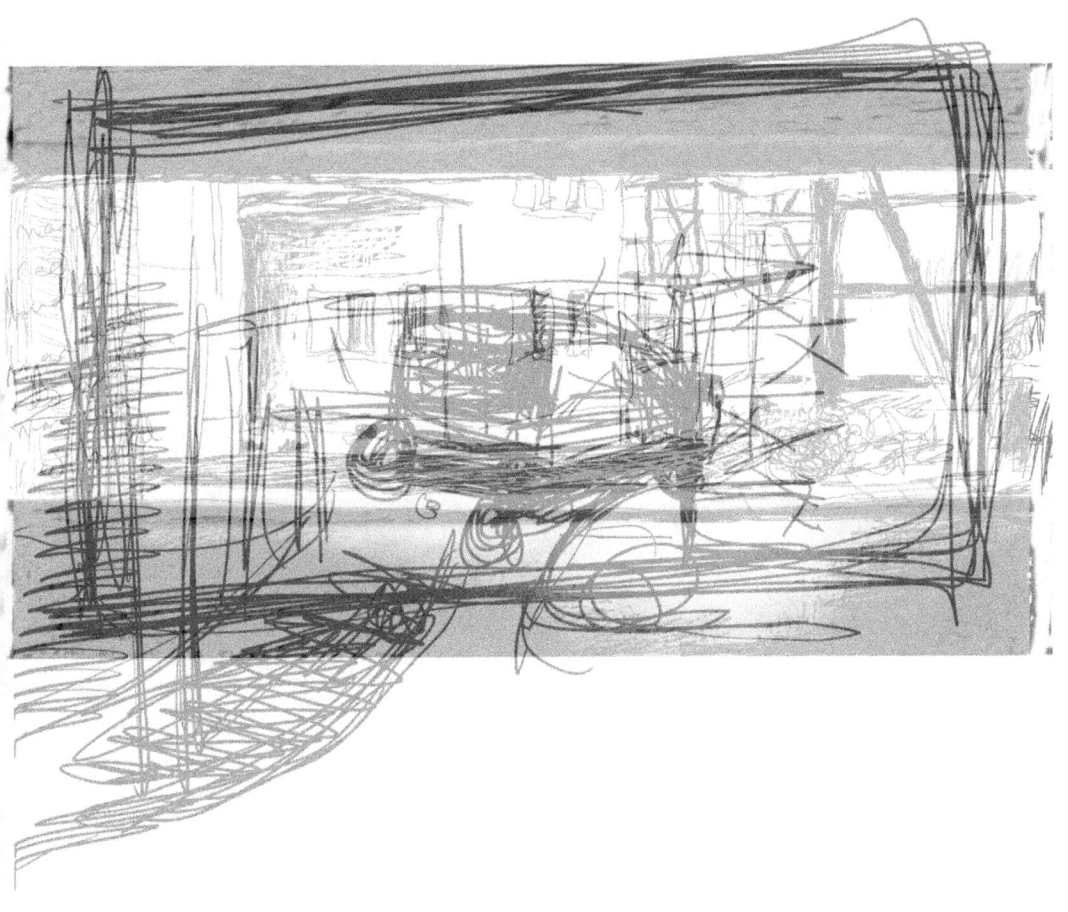

VAN/WAGEN

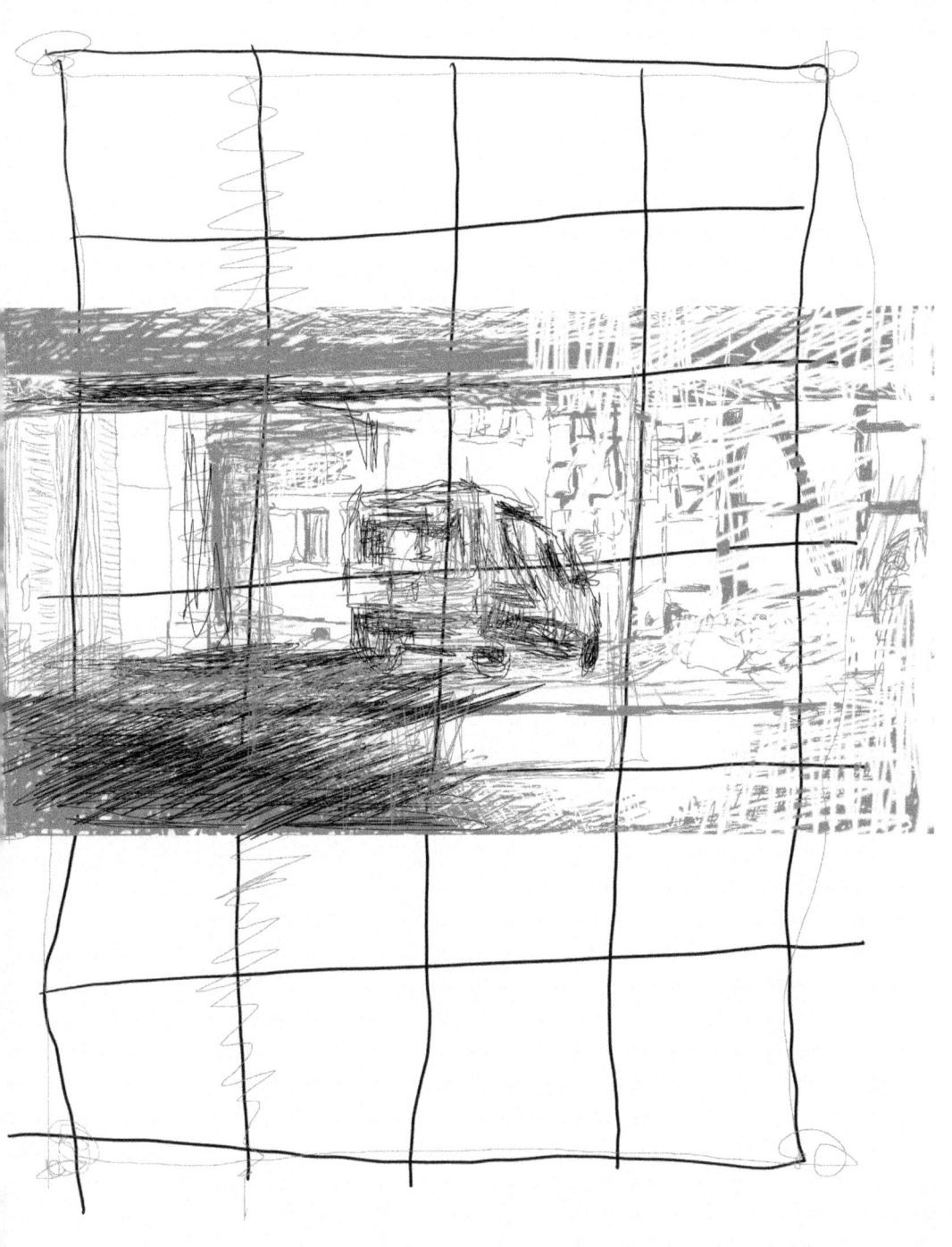

WOMAN WITH GREY HAT/FRAU MIT GRAUEM HUT

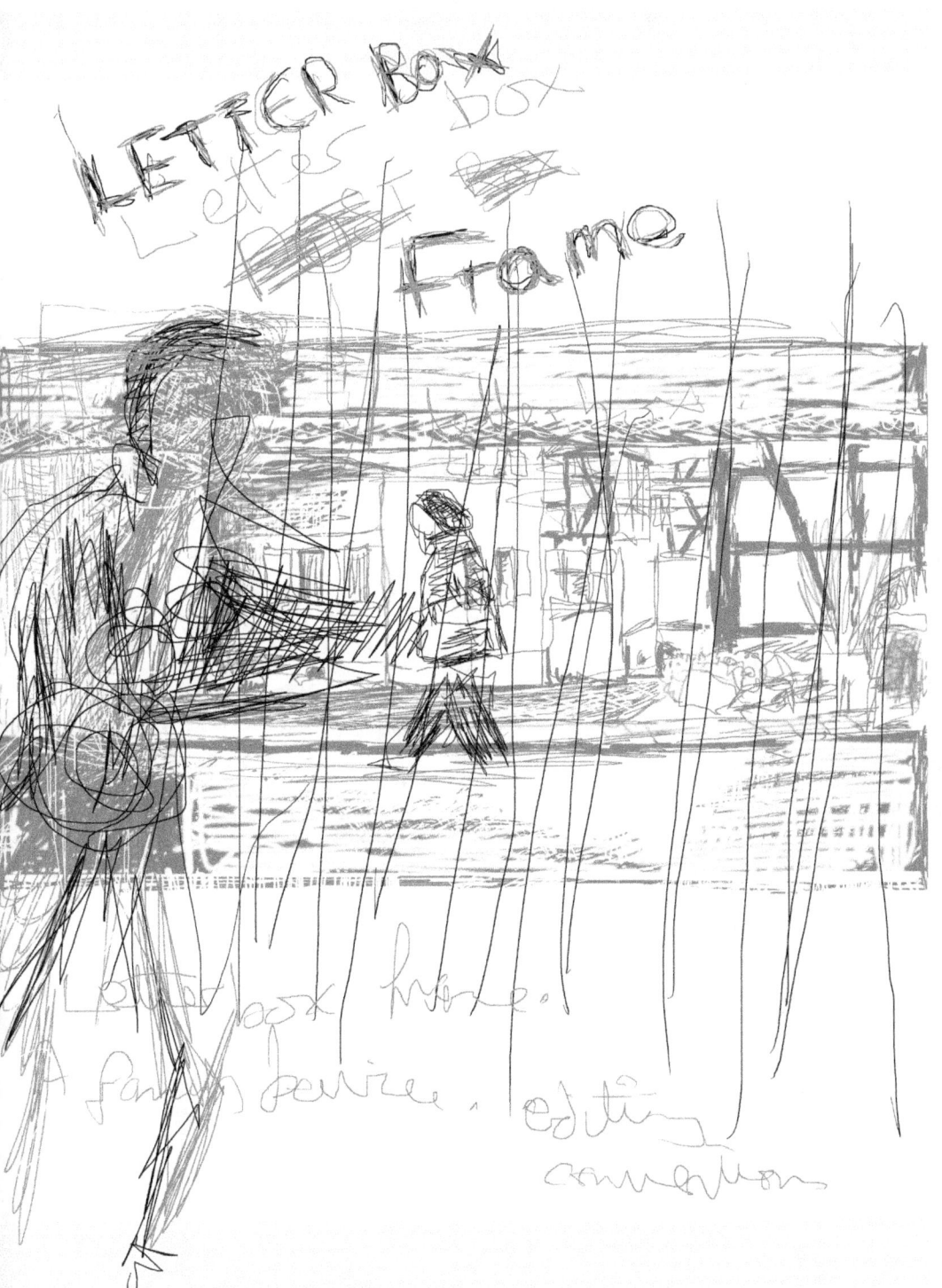

WOMAN WITH GREY HAT/FRAU MIT GRAUEM HUT

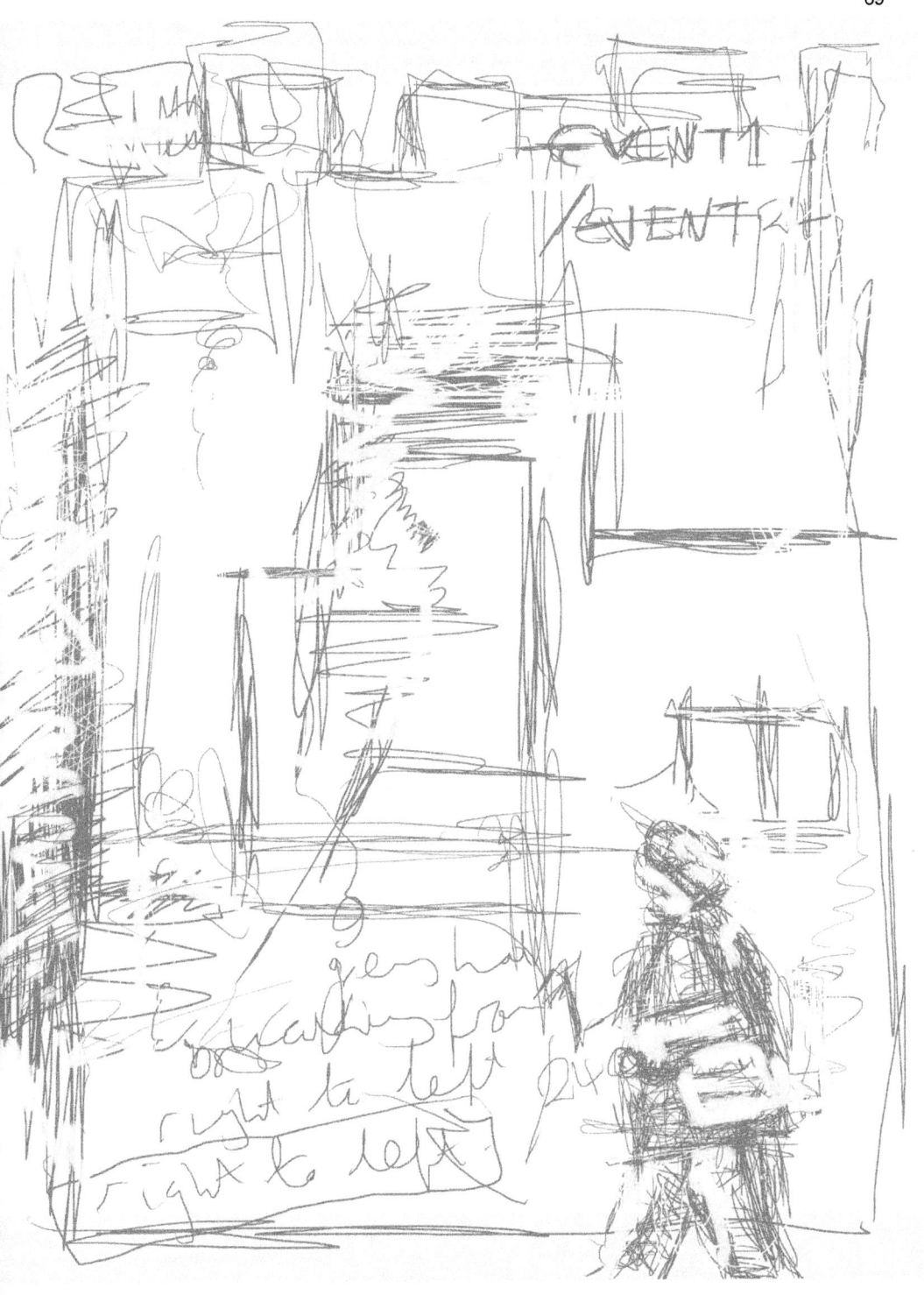

WOMAN WITH GREY HAT/FRAU MIT GRAUEM HUT

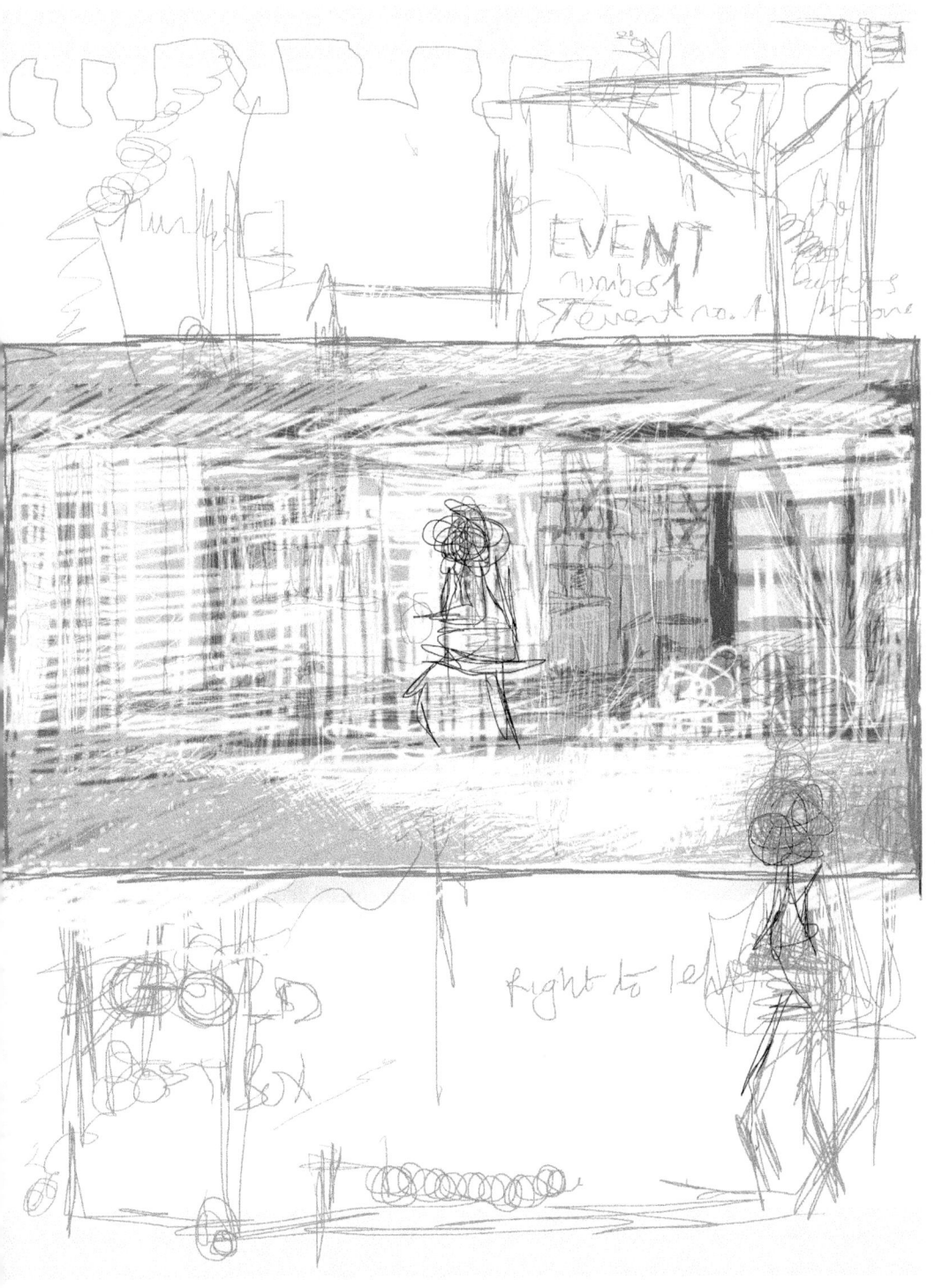

MOVING PLASTIC/PLASTIK BEWEGT SICH

73

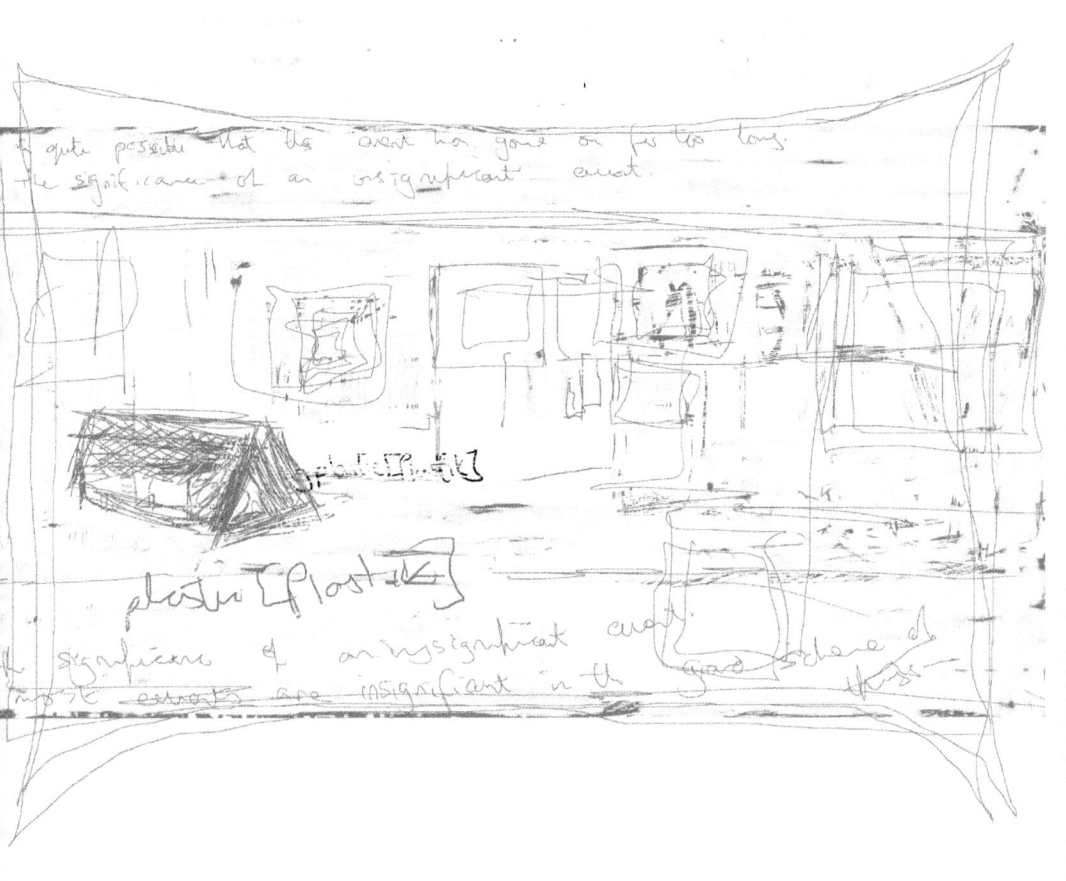

plastic [Plastik]

MOVING PLASTIC/PLASTIK BEWEGT SICH

In a still ~~image~~ image, taken from a static video image, of something insignificant, like some plastic [Plastik] moving in the wind, moves slightly and becomes an 'event'. where the event becomes living and endless. The 'origin of presence' [Derrida] is insignificant but the iterations becomes significant. Where the editing contributes more than the original. ~~~~. Iterability is infinite and ∴ much more significant.

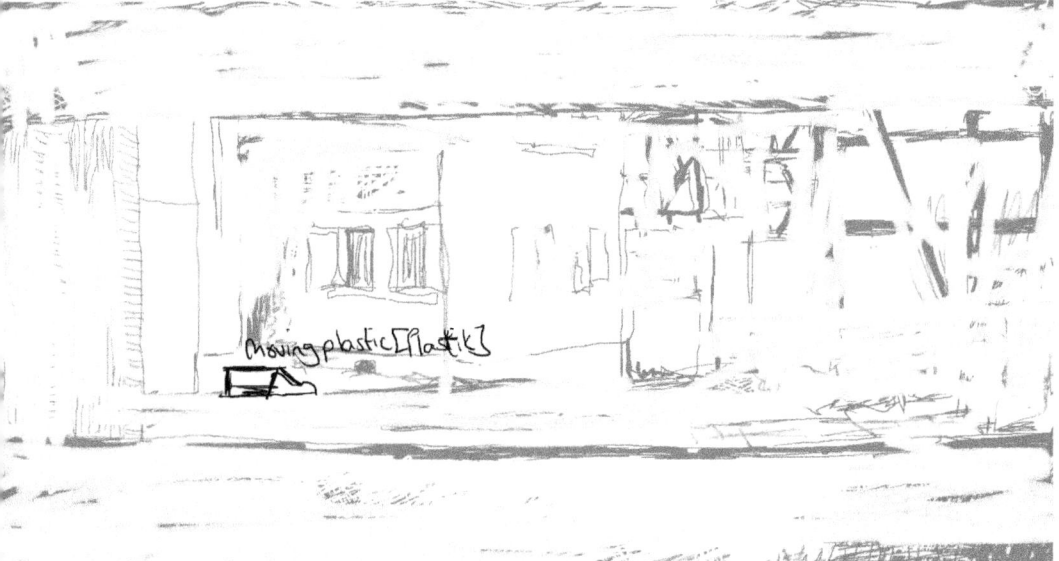

moving plastic [Plastik]

In a still ~~image~~ image, taken from a static video image, of something insignificant, like some plastic [Plastik] moving in the wind, moves slightly and becomes an 'event'. where the event becomes living and endless. The 'origin of presence' [Derrida] is insignificant but the iterations becomes significant. Where the editing contributes more than the original. ~~~~. Iterability is infinite and ∴ much more significant.

MOVING PLASTIC/PLASTIK BEWEGT SICH

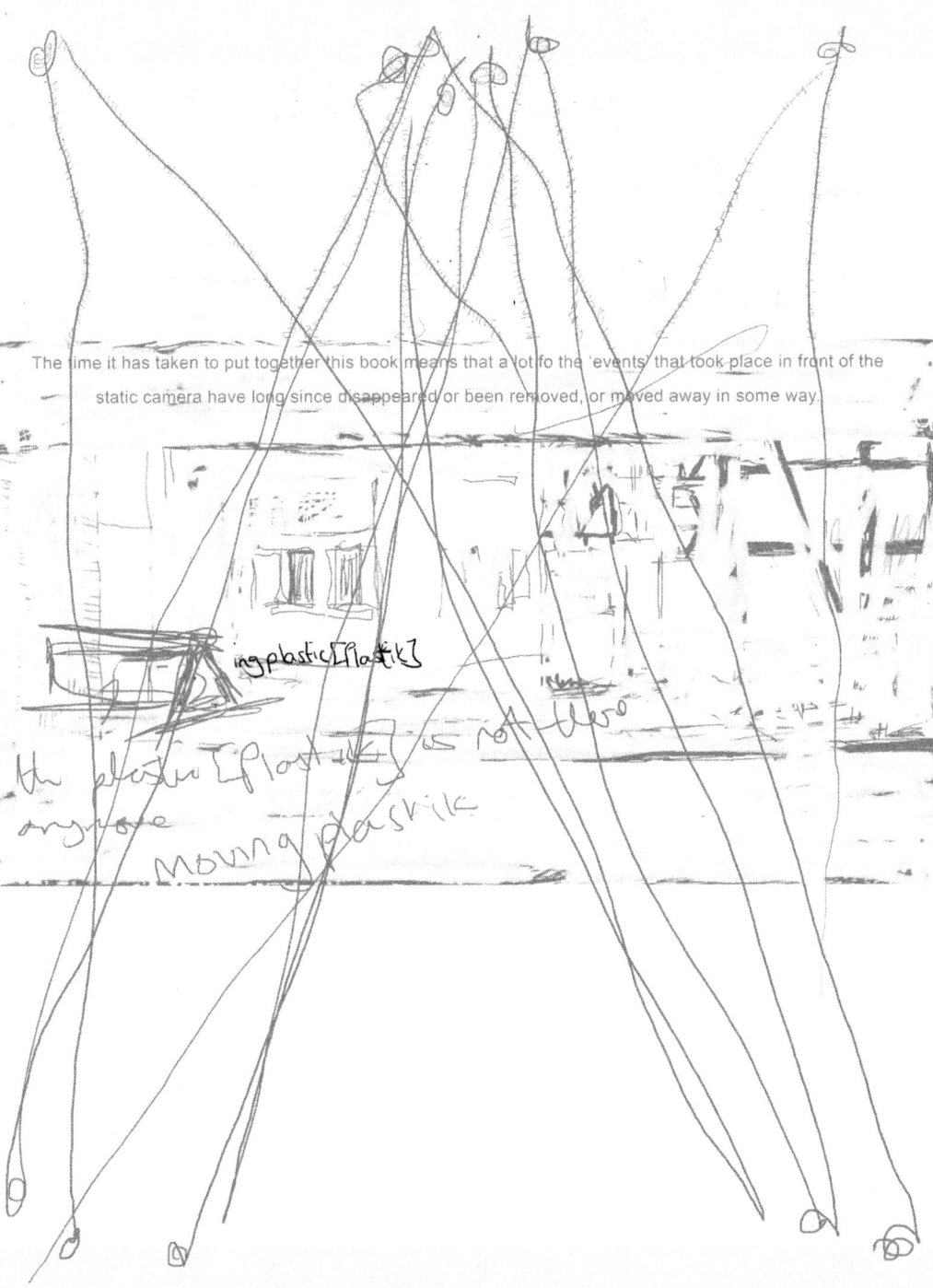

The time it has taken to put together this book means that a lot fo the 'events' that took place in front of the static camera have long since disappeared or been removed, or moved away in some way.

ingplastic[Plastik]

the plastic [Plastik] is not there anymore

moving plastik

WOMAN IN JEANS/FRAU IN JEANS

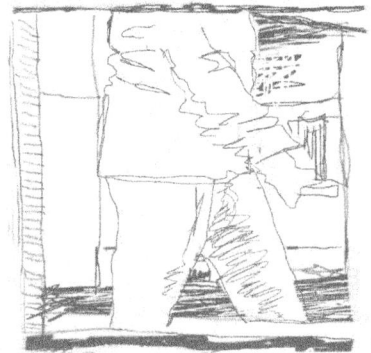

WOMAN IN JEANS/FRAU IN JEANS

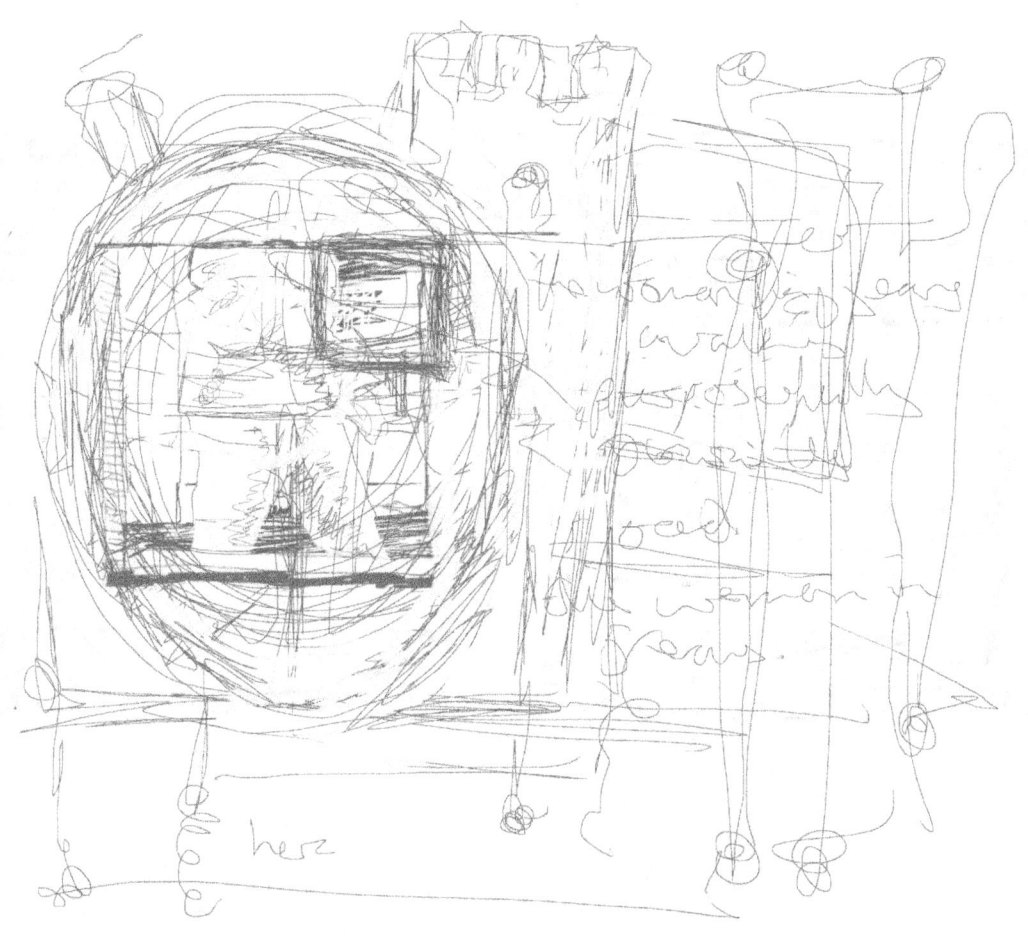

82

WOMAN IN JEANS/FRAU IN JEANS

letterbox

The letterbox begins the edits process and the drawings CONTINUE this process. The end point is publishing.

There is a clear beginning, middle and end to the process but the events taking place in front of the camera have no such beginning, middle and end. Even if each event is considered as a narrative, the information available is cropped, just like the image. It is cropped by the fixed camera which doesn't follow each subject and by the letterbox which can only open so far and see so much. Where the people/cars/cats come from and go to remain a mystery. My assumption is that they are all local and live interesting lives— especially the cats.

WOMAN IN JEANS/FRAU IN JEANS

woman in jeans woman in jeans woman in jeans woman in jeans woman in jeans woman in jeans woman in jeans woman in jeans woman in

woman in jeans woman in jeans woman in jeans woman in jeans woman in jeans woman in jeans woman in jeans woman in jeans woman in

WOMAN IN JEANS/FRAU IN JEANS

It's the end of March and it's not started to get warmer yet. She's wearing one of those puffy jackets that people like. The thoughts passing through her head as she walk past can only be imagined. I like to think that she is planning to spend her afternoon drawing and she is thinking about something related to that. She might be considering how to get her repeated visual motif to progress, because it only seems to move on once she has resolved something about it. It is a persistant bugger otherwise. She might be thinking about the different framing devices that she has used and how to present these and the dilemmas they have caused. She might be thinking about whether a digital image has any kind of sustainability in terms of medium, and whether it will become obsolete at some point in the near future. She might be thinking about the thinking hand, and how drawing can be a useful method for thinking through problems, not just visual problems related to the drawing itself but conceiptual problems related to the wider context of the work. She might be considering her source material being a moving image, digital video, and how that capturing this image with a static camera, making it into a still image and then ediitng it with drawing creates a sense of series or movement that retains some of the sequential nature of video. I'm sure she's thinking about that.

static camera moving subject
still image

continuing her journey.
walking from left to right.

LATER DARK CAR/SPÄTES DUNKLES AUTO

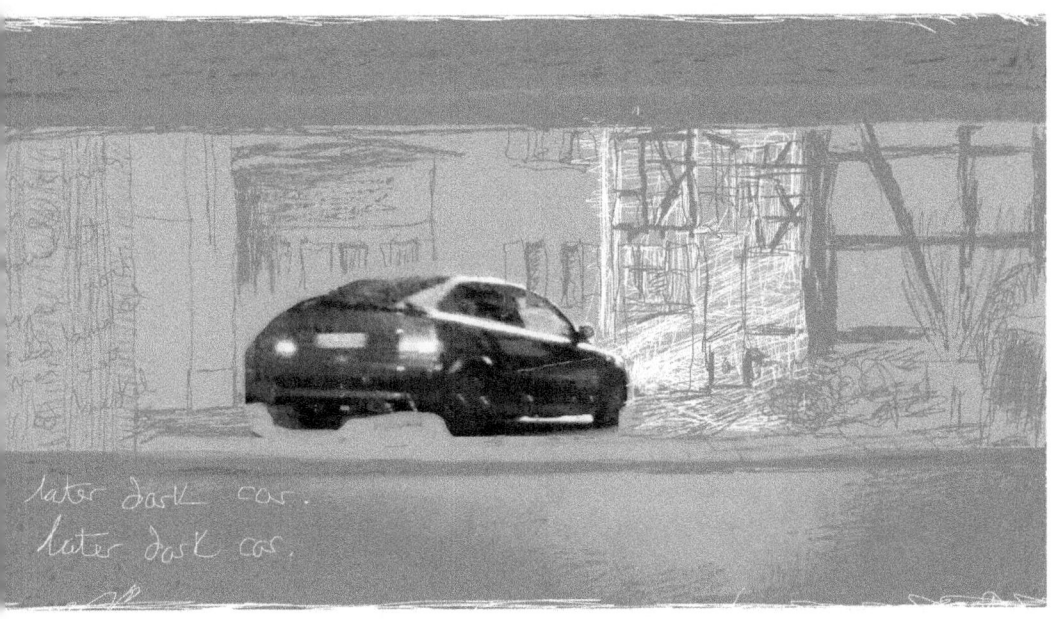

later dark car.
later dark car.

LATER DARK CAR/SPÄTES DUNKLES AUTO

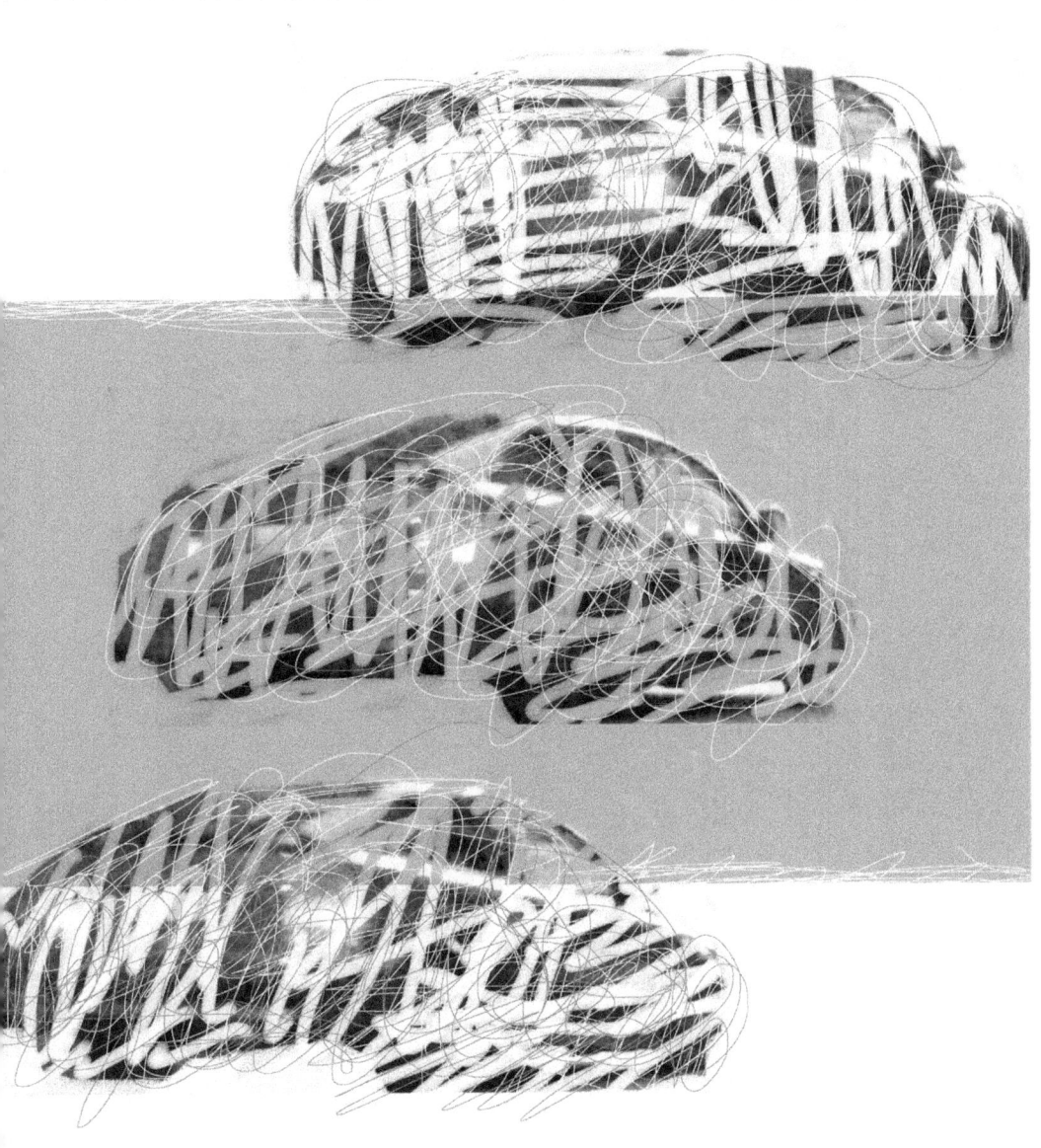

LATER DARK CAR/SPÄTES DUNKLES AUTO

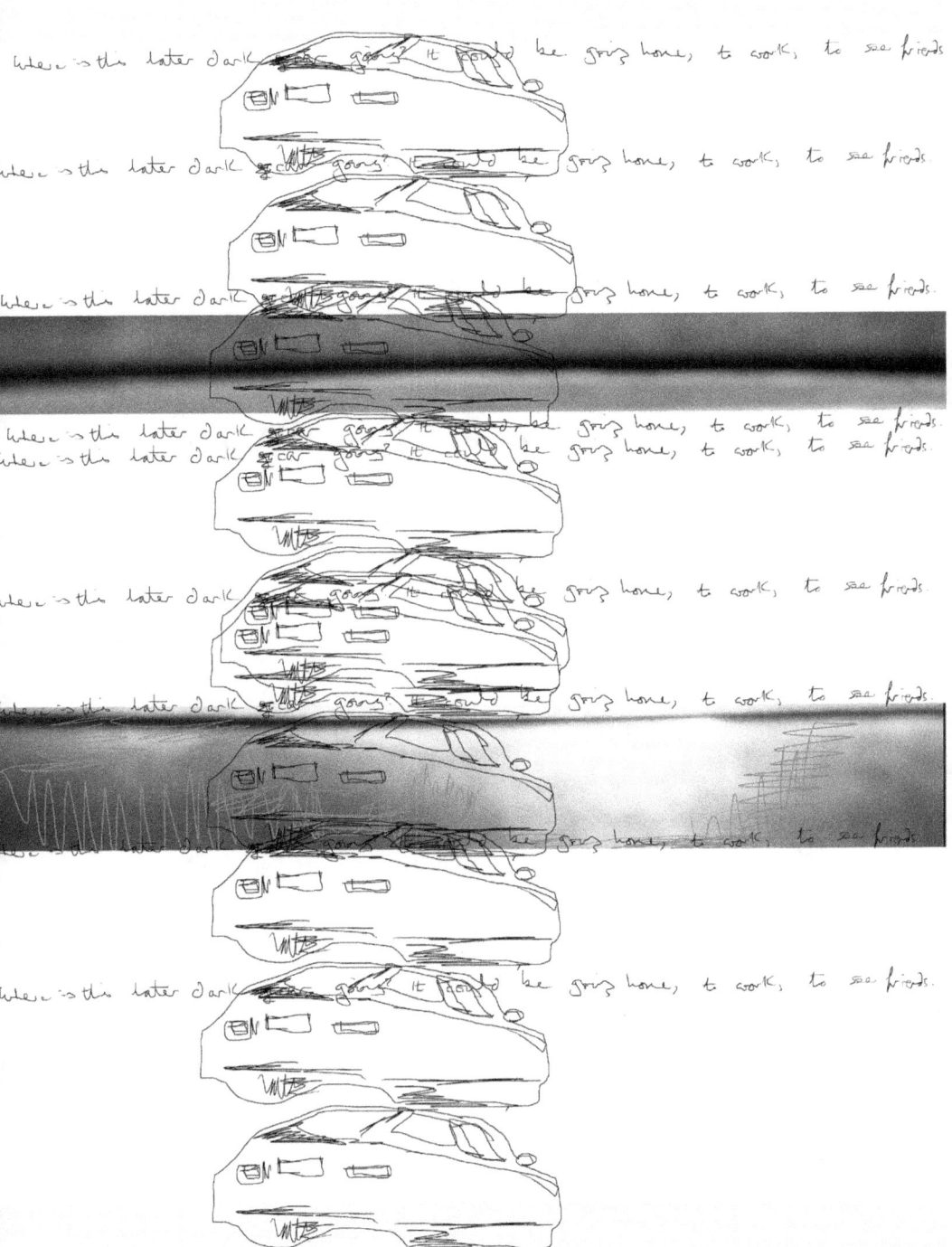

where is this later dark car going? It could be going home, to work, to see friends

where is this later dark car going? It could be going home, to work, to see friends

where is this later dark car going? It could be going home, to work, to see friends.

where is this later dark car going? It could be going home, to work, to see friends.
where is this later dark car going? It could be going home, to work, to see friends.

where is this later dark car going? It could be going home, to work, to see friends.

where is this later dark car going? It could be going home, to work, to see friends.

where is this later dark car going? It could be going home, to work, to see friends.

where is this later dark car going? It could be going home, to work, to see friends.

LATER DARK CAR/SPÄTES DUNKLES AUTO

LATER DARK CAR/SPÄTES DUNKLES AUTO

I always found it very complicated to drive at night. It was all ok in the city, where there were street lights, but in the countryside it was difficult to judge when to dip your lights and to remember to put them back on full beam. I haven't had the opportunity to drive in Germany yet. Driving n the right side of the road is one thing, but I haven't driven a car in approximately ten years so the thought of doing it it a bit daunting.

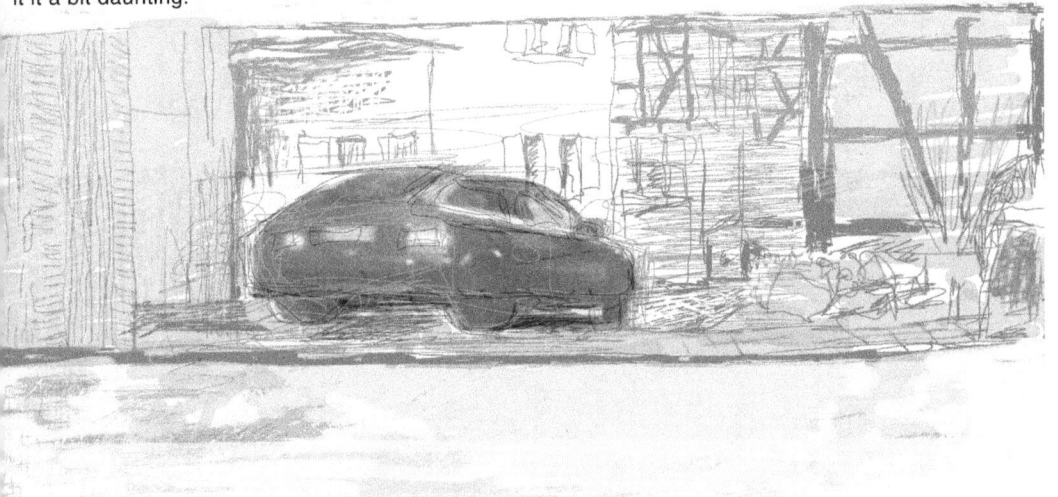

Driving is a good way to explore the countryside though, at the moment I am limited to visiting small towns that are either on a train or bus route. There are many places that I can't get to. I want to explore the area and get to know all of the towns. There is a lot of history and some very beautiful scenery that I am missing out on. However, I like not owning a car, and I love taking the train, so it's six of one and half a dozen of the other.

PARENT AND CHILD/ELTERNTEIL MIT KIND

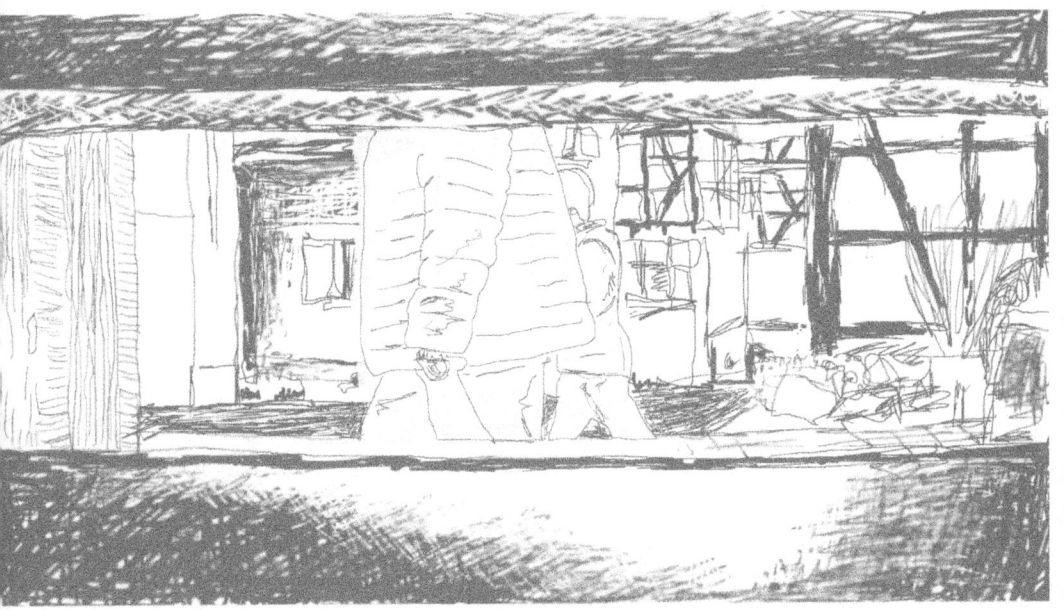

PARENT AND CHILD/ELTERNTEIL MIT KIND

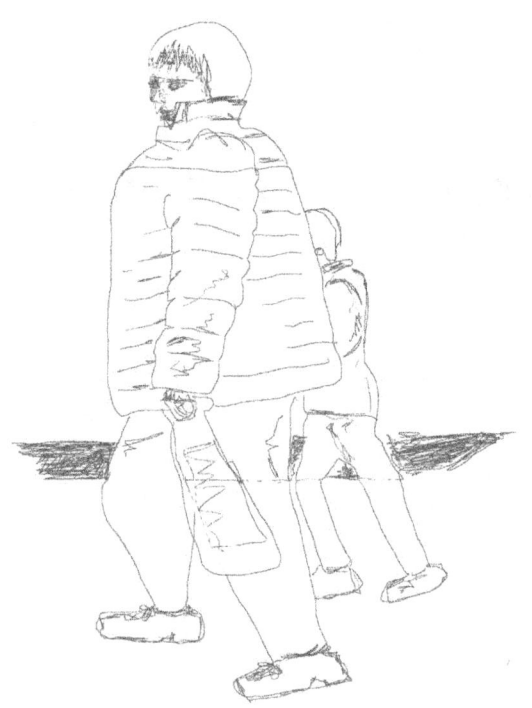

PARENT AND CHILD/ELTERNTEIL MIT KIND

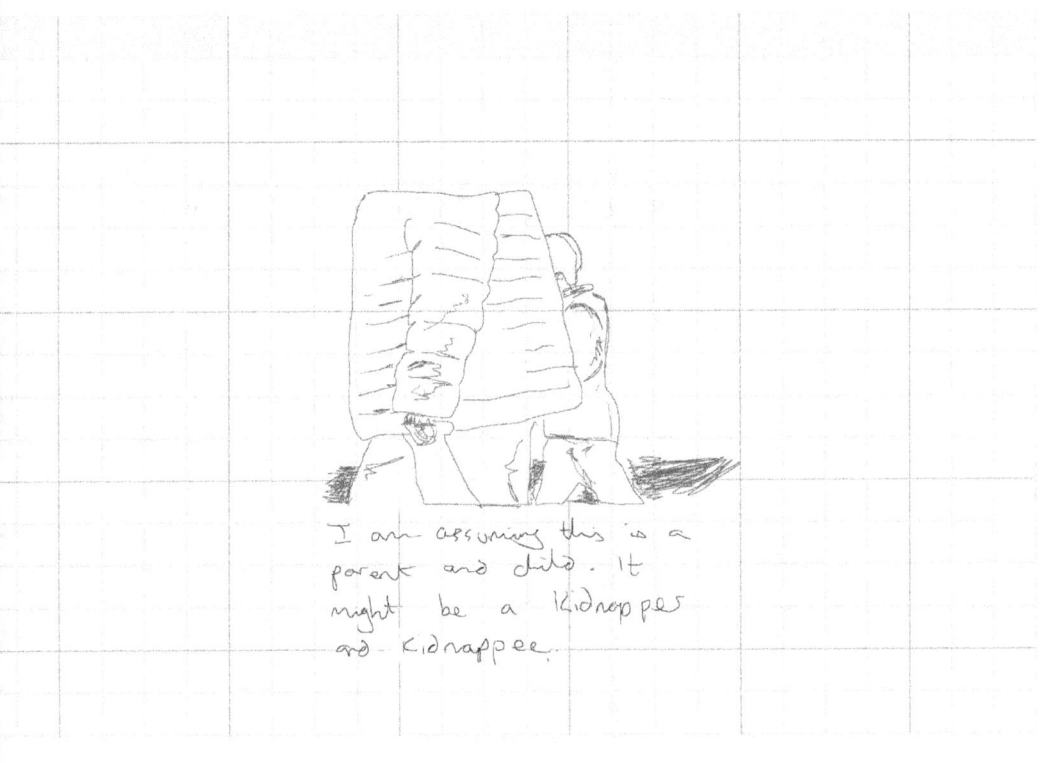

I am assuming this is a
parent and child. It
might be a kidnapper
and kidnappee.

PARENT AND CHILD/ELTERNTEIL MIT KIND

THE PURPOSE OF THE CHILD IS NOT CLEAR
THE PURPOSE OF THE CHILD IS NOT CLEAR
THE PURPOSE OF THE CHILD IS NOT CLEAR
THE PURPOSE OF THE CHILD IS NOT CLEAR
THE PURPOSE OF THE CHILD IS NOT CLEAR
THE PURPOSE OF THE CHILD IS NOT CLEAR
THE PURPOSE OF THE CHILD IS NOT CLEAR
THE PURPOSE OF THE CHILD IS NOT CLEAR
THE PURPOSE OF THE CHILD IS NOT CLEAR
THE PURPOSE OF THE CHILD IS NOT CLEAR
THE PURPOSE OF THE CHILD IS NOT CLEAR
THE PURPOSE OF THE CHILD IS NOT CLEAR
THE PURPOSE OF THE CHILD IS NOT CLEAR
THE PURPOSE OF THE CHILD IS NOT CLEAR
THE PURPOSE OF THE CHILD IS NOT CLEAR
THE PURPOSE OF THE CHILD IS NOT CLEAR
THE PURPOSE OF THE CHILD IS NOT CLEAR
THE PURPOSE OF THE CHILD IS NOT CLEAR
THE PURPOSE OF THE CHILD IS NOT CLEAR
THE PURPOSE OF THE CHILD IS NOT CLEAR

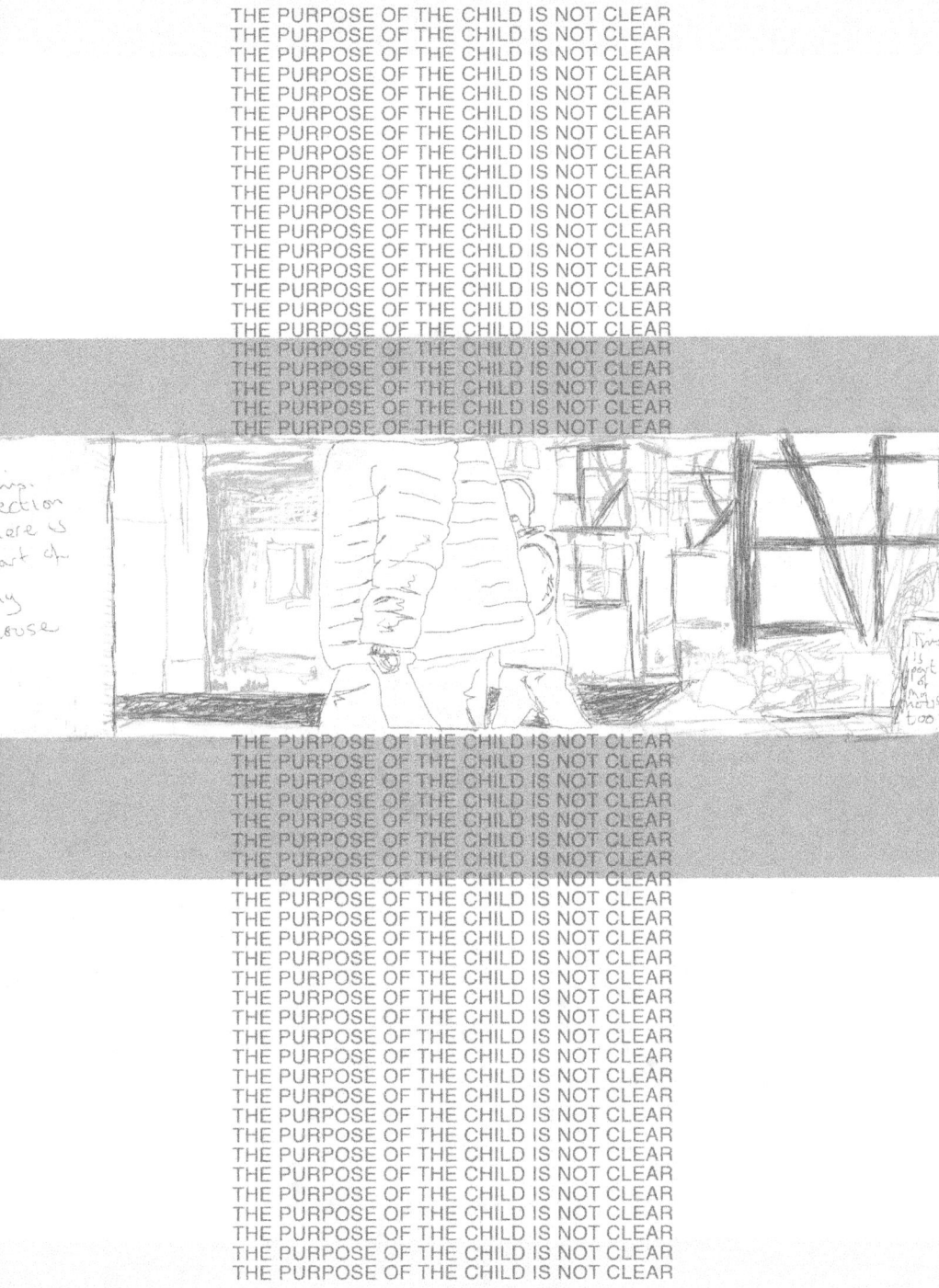

THE PURPOSE OF THE CHILD IS NOT CLEAR
THE PURPOSE OF THE CHILD IS NOT CLEAR
THE PURPOSE OF THE CHILD IS NOT CLEAR
THE PURPOSE OF THE CHILD IS NOT CLEAR
THE PURPOSE OF THE CHILD IS NOT CLEAR
THE PURPOSE OF THE CHILD IS NOT CLEAR
THE PURPOSE OF THE CHILD IS NOT CLEAR
THE PURPOSE OF THE CHILD IS NOT CLEAR
THE PURPOSE OF THE CHILD IS NOT CLEAR
THE PURPOSE OF THE CHILD IS NOT CLEAR
THE PURPOSE OF THE CHILD IS NOT CLEAR
THE PURPOSE OF THE CHILD IS NOT CLEAR
THE PURPOSE OF THE CHILD IS NOT CLEAR
THE PURPOSE OF THE CHILD IS NOT CLEAR
THE PURPOSE OF THE CHILD IS NOT CLEAR
THE PURPOSE OF THE CHILD IS NOT CLEAR
THE PURPOSE OF THE CHILD IS NOT CLEAR
THE PURPOSE OF THE CHILD IS NOT CLEAR
THE PURPOSE OF THE CHILD IS NOT CLEAR
THE PURPOSE OF THE CHILD IS NOT CLEAR
THE PURPOSE OF THE CHILD IS NOT CLEAR
THE PURPOSE OF THE CHILD IS NOT CLEAR
THE PURPOSE OF THE CHILD IS NOT CLEAR

PARENT AND CHILD/ELTERNTEIL MIT KIND

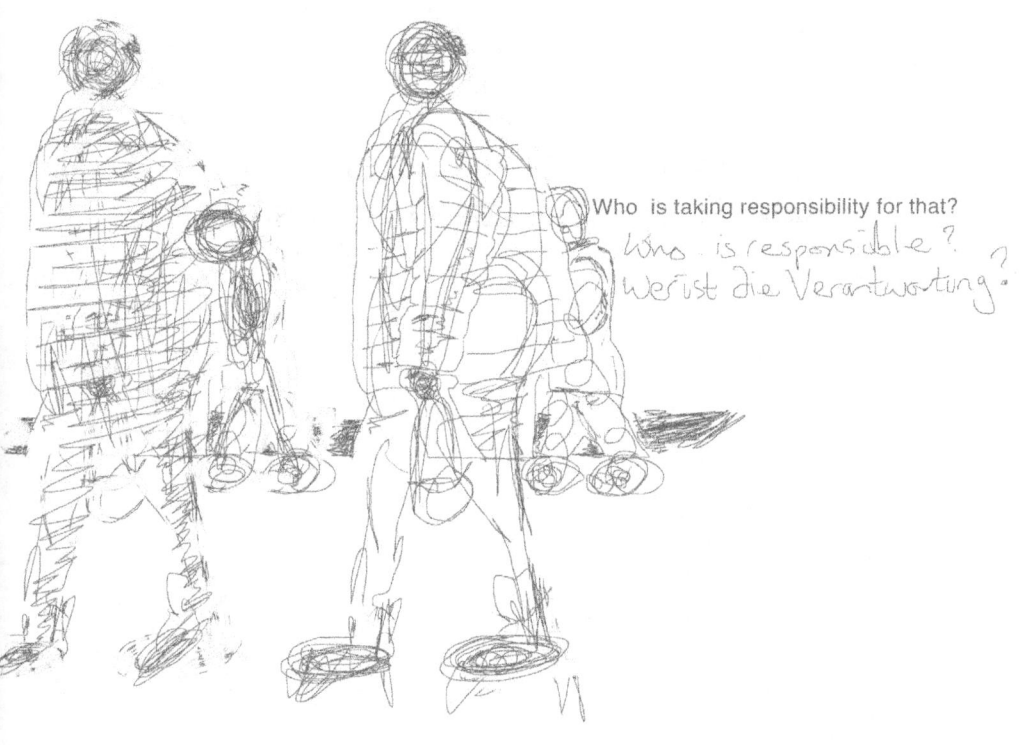

Who is taking responsibility for that?

Who is responsible?
Wer ist die Verantwortung?

**MAN WITH COAT OVER HIS SHOULDER/
MANN MIT MANTEL ÜBER DER SCHULTER**

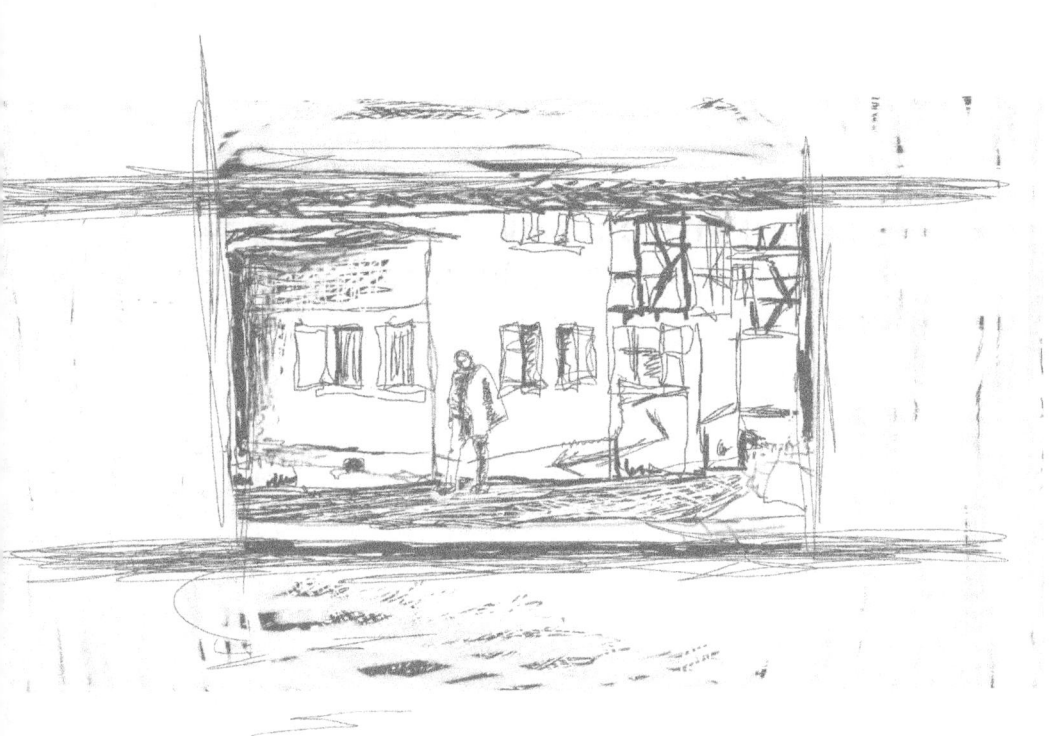

the man with the coat over his shoulder walks up the
street as he is probably going to the car which
is parked in the carpark at the top of
the hill next to my house.

**MAN WITH COAT OVER HIS SHOULDER/
MANN MIT MANTEL ÜBER DER SCHULTER**

**MAN WITH COAT OVER HIS SHOULDER/
MANN MIT MANTEL ÜBER DER SCHULTER**

and the man carried his goat in such a way that he looked like he was going off to conquer something. He was probably just going to collect his car from the car park.

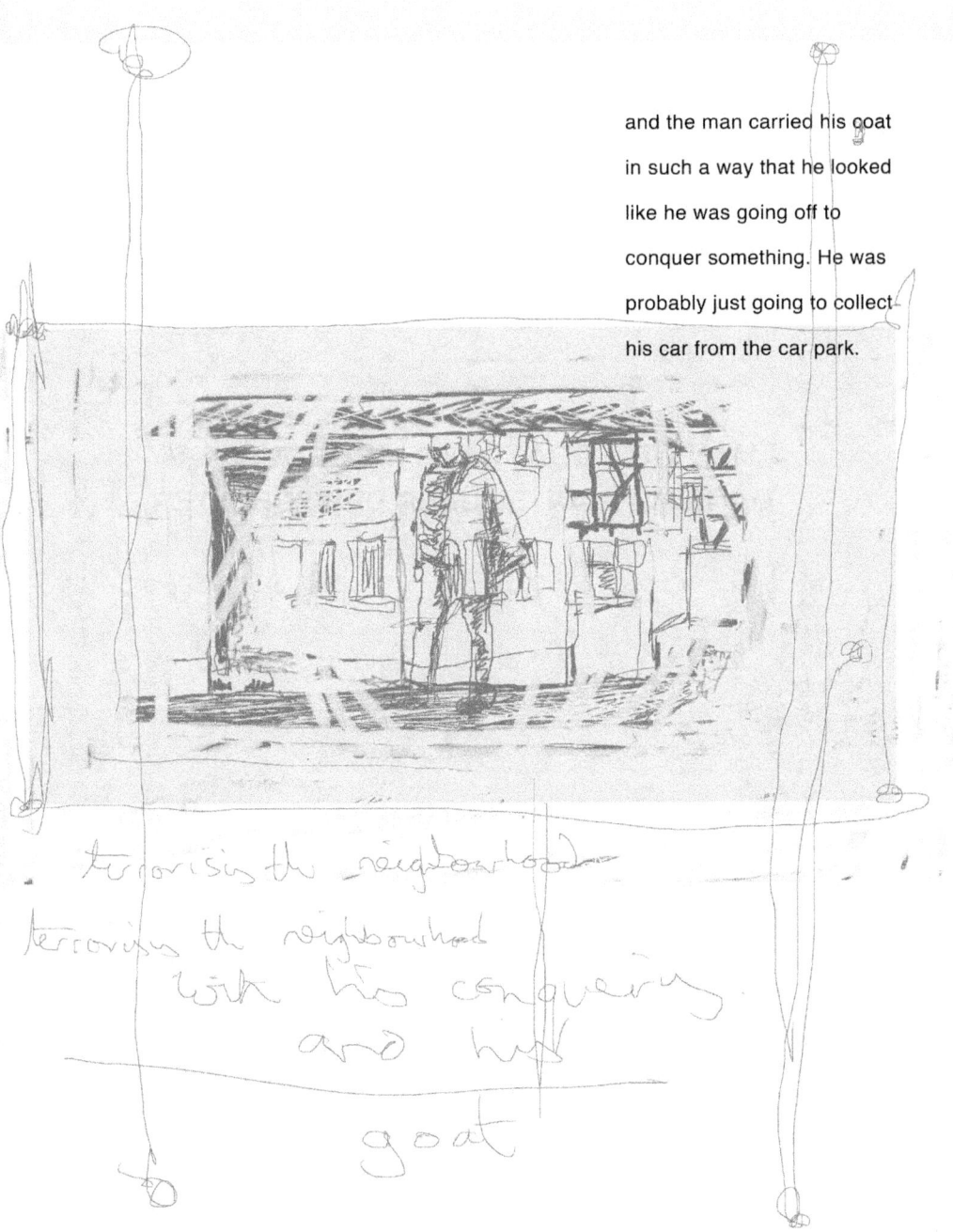

terrorising the neighbourhood
terrorising the neighbourhood
with his conquering
and his
goat

**MAN WITH COAT OVER HIS SHOULDER/
MANN MIT MANTEL ÜBER DER SCHULTER**

the man with the coat over his shoulder

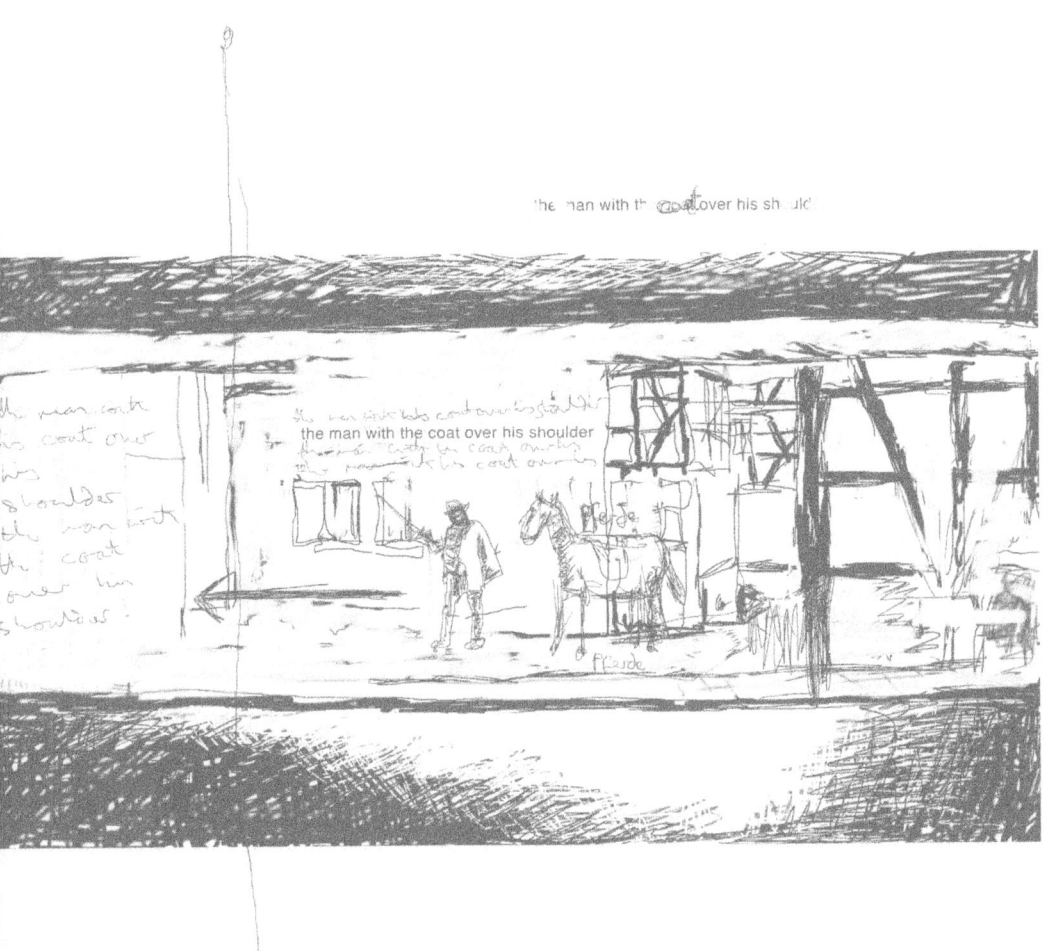

the man with the coat over his shoulder

**MAN WITH COAT OVER HIS SHOULDER/
MANN MIT MANTEL ÜBER DER SCHULTER**

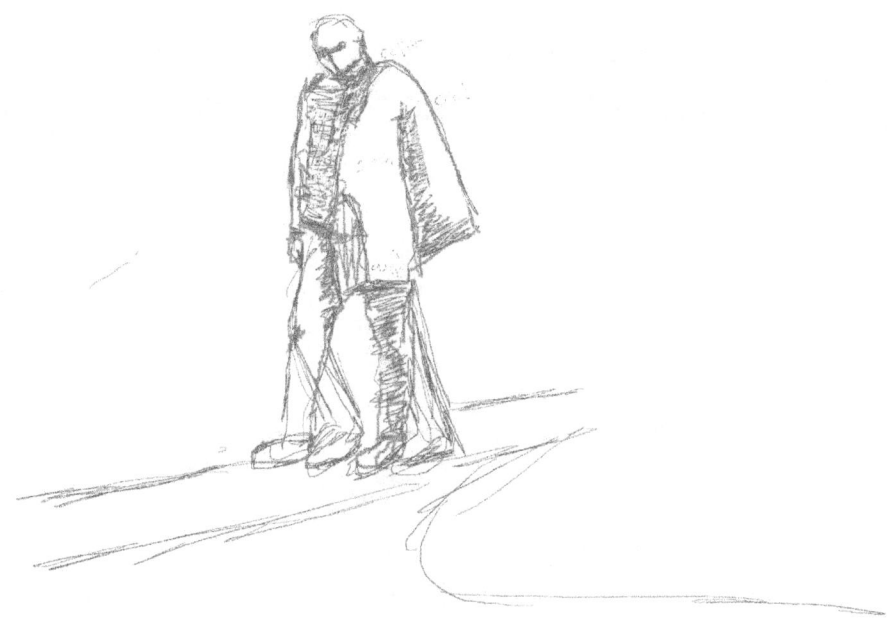

DIFFERENT ROUTE BLACK CAT/
SCHWARZE KATZE SCHLÄGT EINEN ANDEREN WEG EIN

You can't see the small
black cat because it's dark
and the cat is behind
a bush. But I promise
that there is a small
black cat in the video.

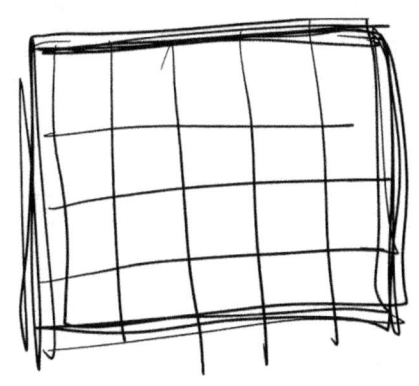

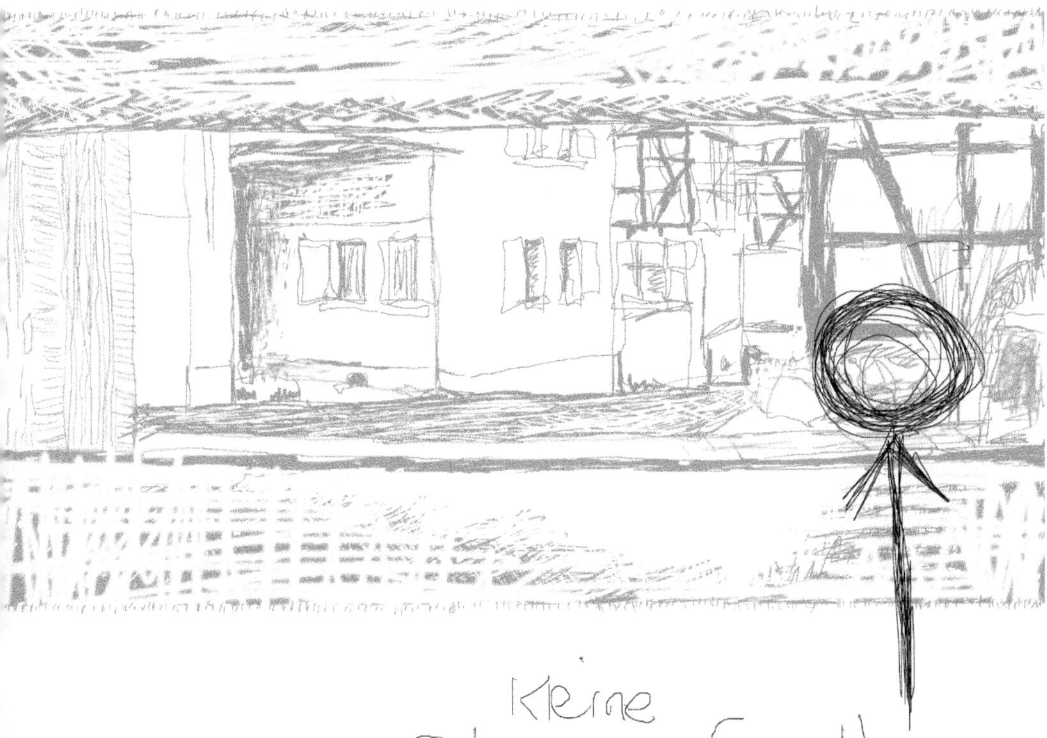

Kleine
Schwarze   Small
Katze   black
                cat

DIFFERENT ROUTE BLACK CAT/
SCHWARZE KATZE SCHLÄGT EINEN ANDEREN WEG EIN

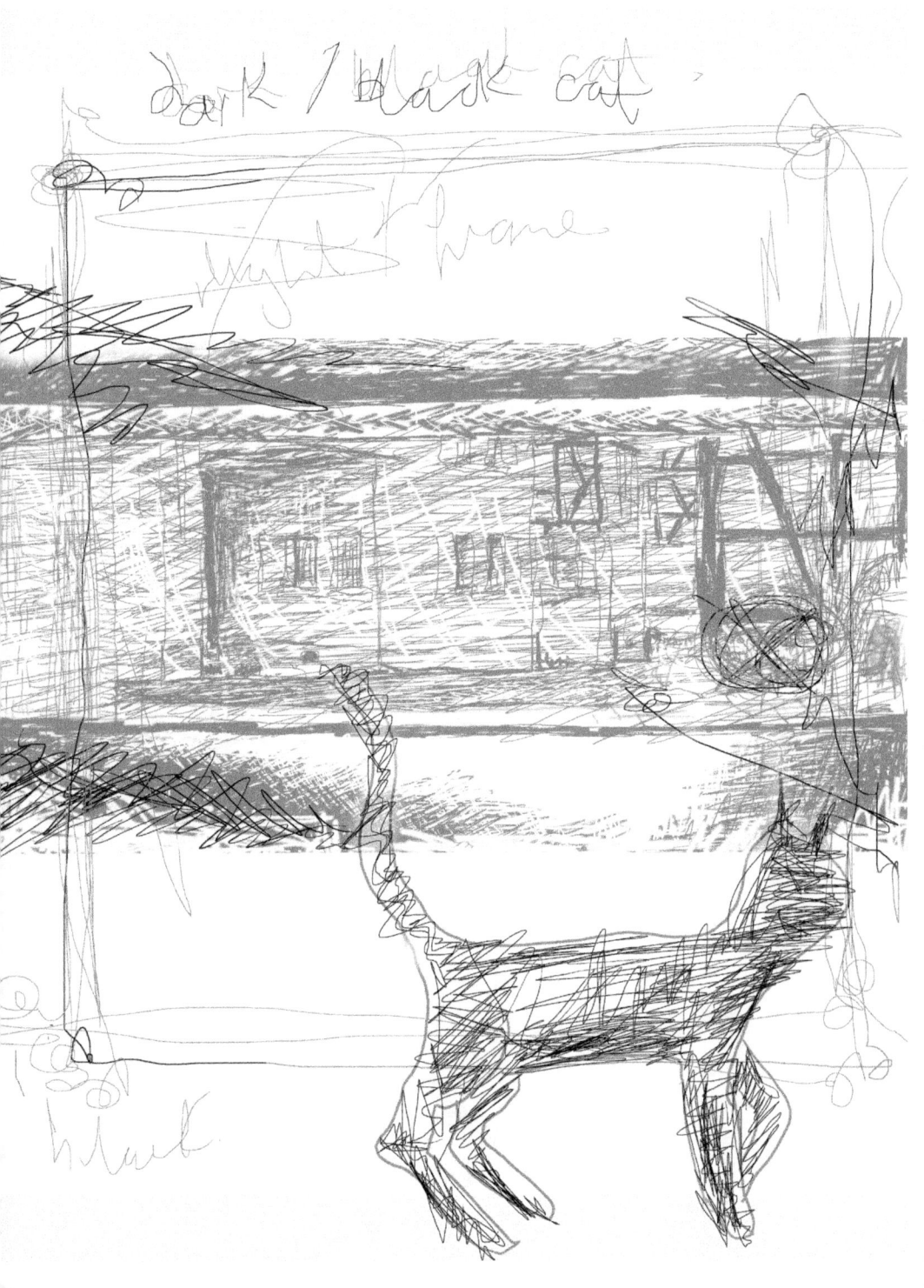

DIFFERENT ROUTE BLACK CAT/
SCHWARZE KATZE SCHLÄGT EINEN ANDEREN WEG EIN

There's a small black cat walking
up the hill. He's moving up, close
to the wall, he's small and
sleek and shiny and black.
He's not old, a young cat
in his prime and he's looking
for something or going somewhere
in particular. He has taken
this route many times,
always the same path, and
he is not worried about
obstructions. Later he will
go home to his warm
cosy house and he will
eat his cat food and
sleep on a warm pile of clothes.

CLOSE UP OF CAR/CLOSE-UP EINES AUTO

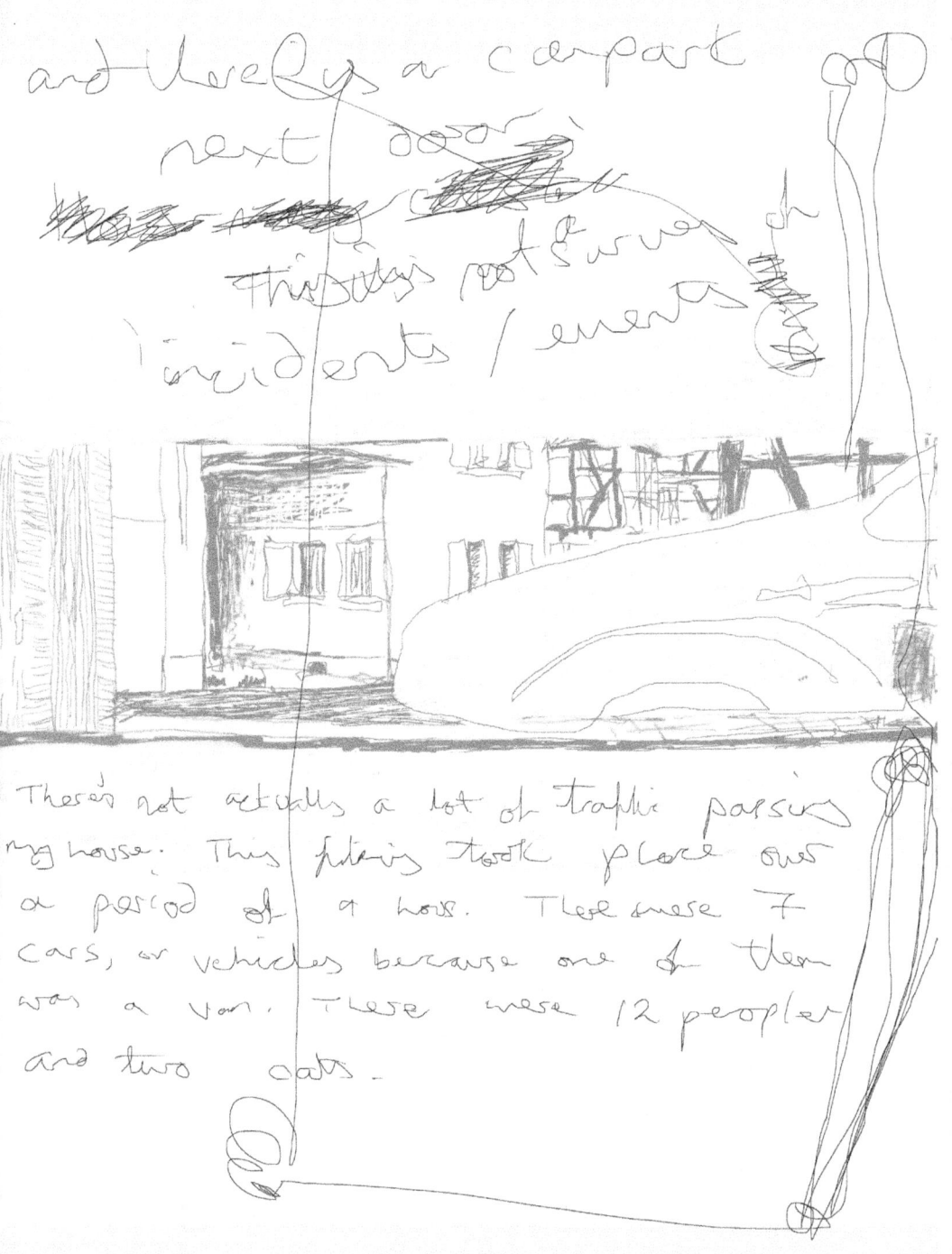

and there's a carpark next door.

This day's not survey incidents / events

There's not actually a lot of traffic passing my house. This photos took place over a period of 4 hours. There were 7 cars, or vehicles because one of them was a van. There were 12 people and two cats.

CLOSE UP OF CAR/CLOSE-UP EINES AUTO

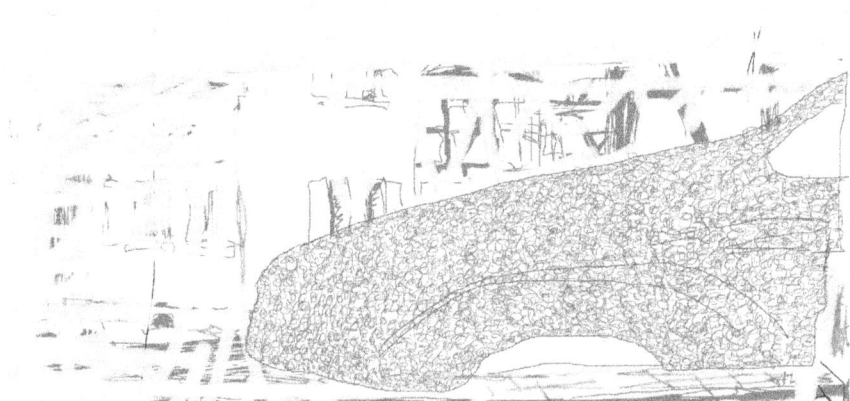

NEIGHBOUR'S CAR/AUTO DES NACHBARN

quite early in the morning. going to work.
ganz früh am Morgen. zur Arbeit gehen.

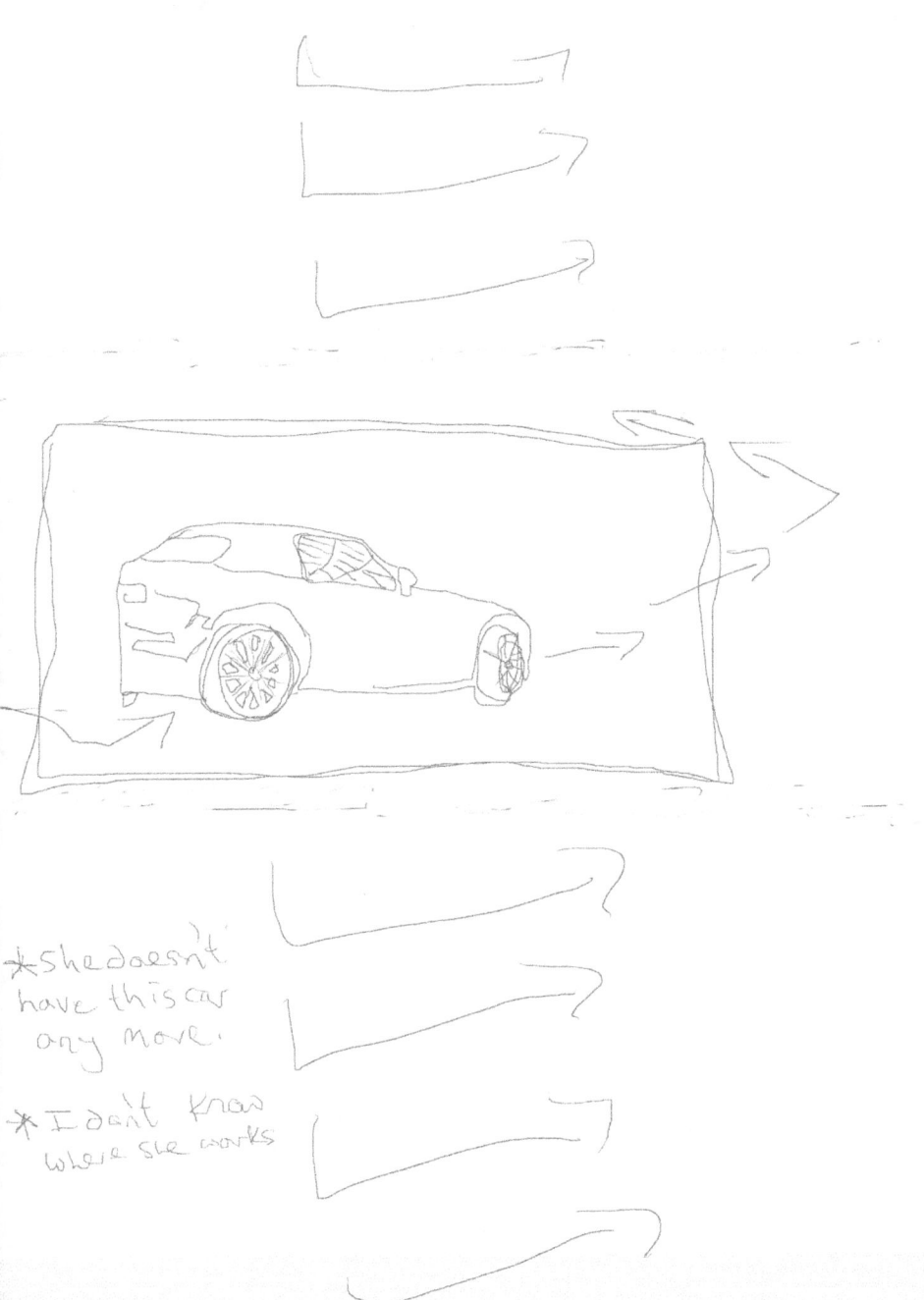

*She doesn't have this car any more.

* I don't know where she works

NEIGHBOUR'S CAR/AUTO DES NACHBARN

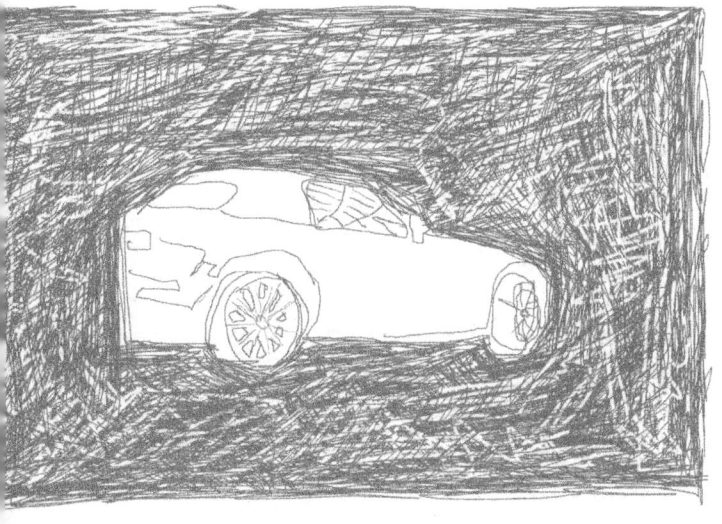

NEIGHBOUR'S CAR/AUTO DES NACHBARN

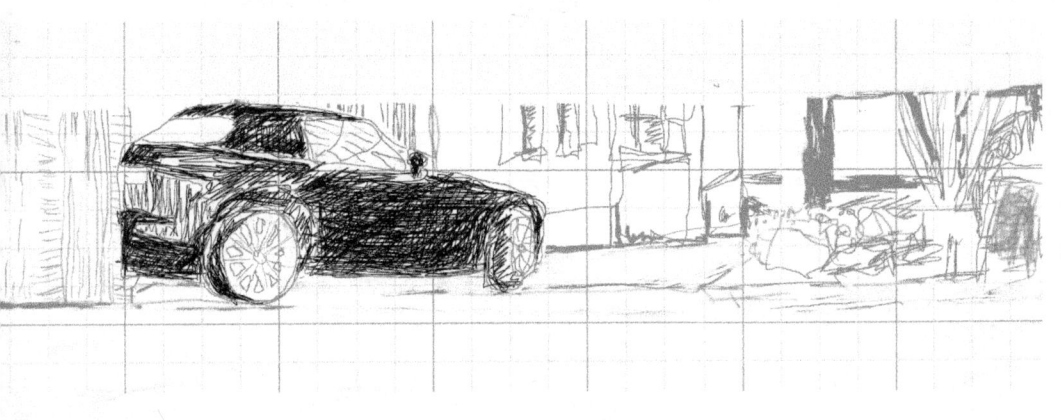

NEIGHBOUR'S CAR/AUTO DES NACHBARN

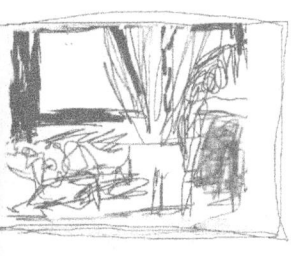

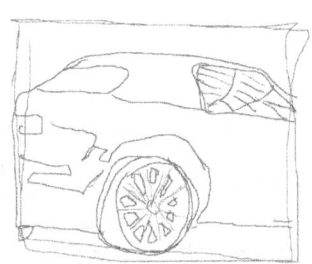

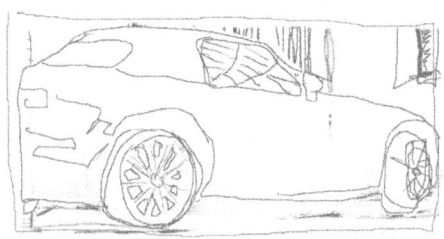

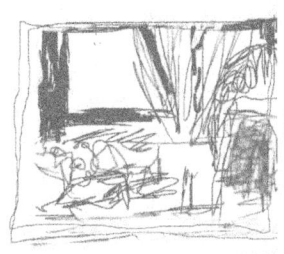

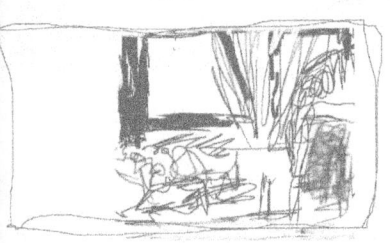

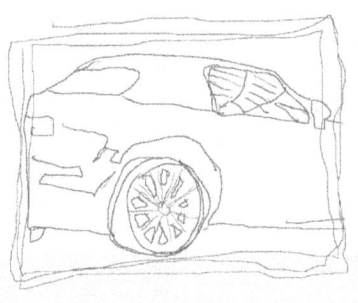

NEIGHBOUR'S CAR/AUTO DES NACHBARN

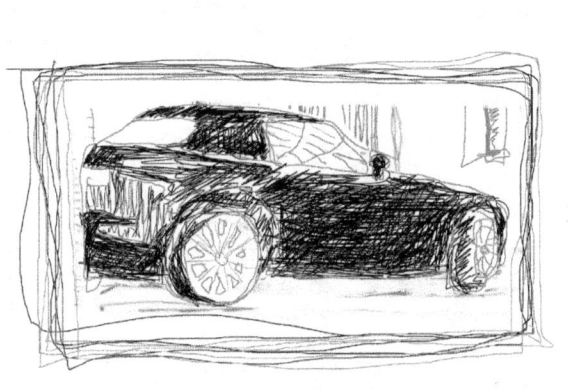

Iteration of an activity leads
to change. editing leads to change.

WOMAN WITH SHOPPING BAG/FRAU MIT EINKAUFSTASCHE

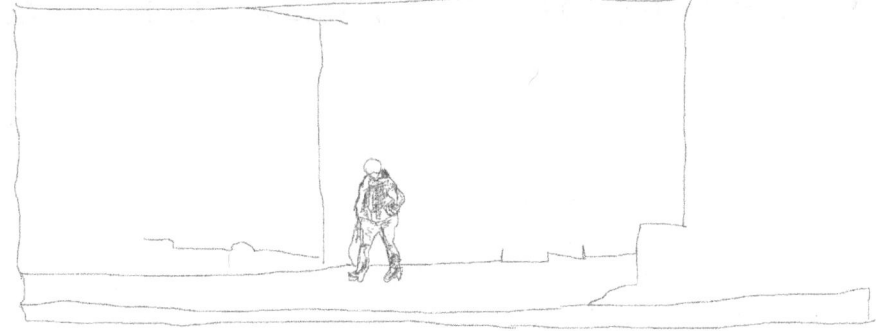

woman with shopping bag

WOMAN WITH SHOPPING BAG/FRAU MIT EINKAUFSTASCHE

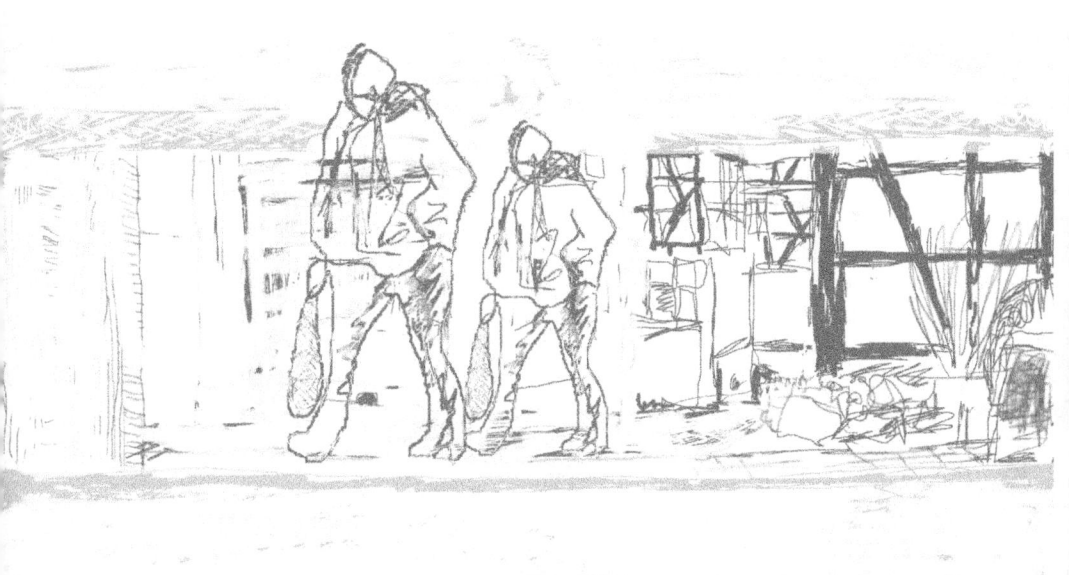

WOMAN WITH SHOPPING BAG/FRAU MIT EINKAUFSTASCHE

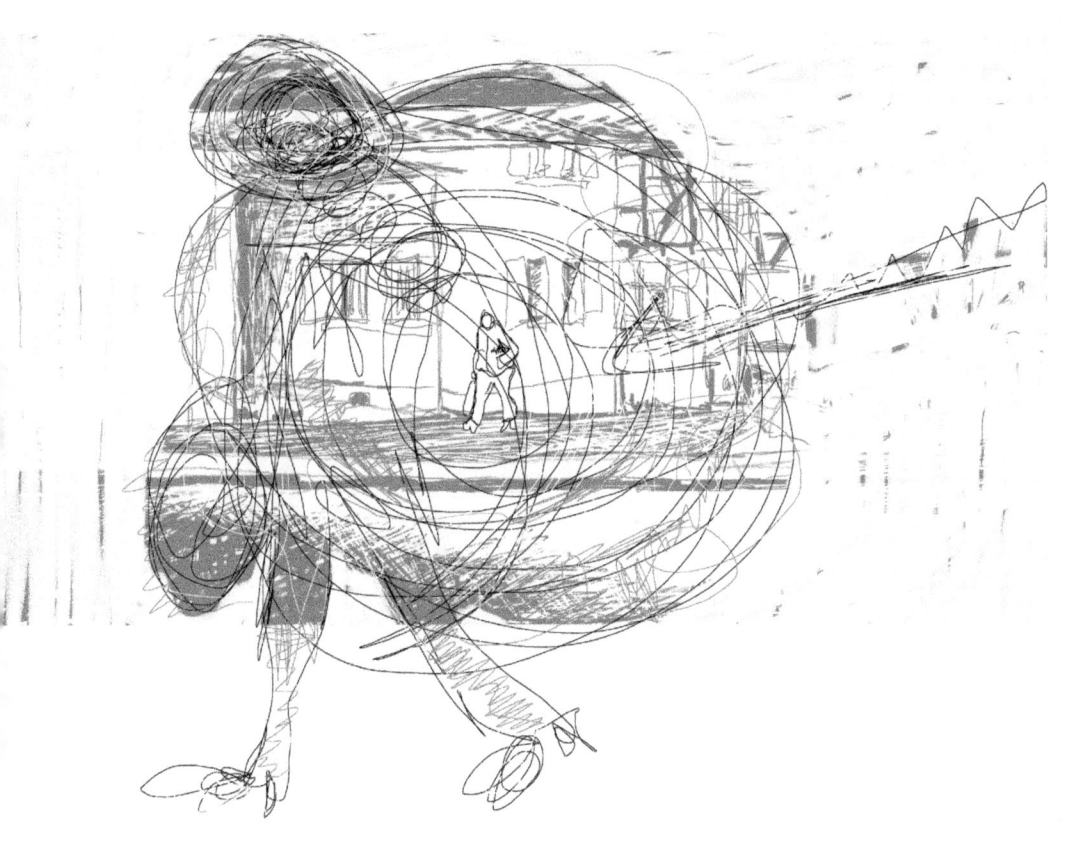

WOMAN WITH SHOPPING BAG/FRAU MIT EINKAUFSTASCHE

Shops in the area include two large supermarkets, several bakers shops (at least three), two shoe shops, at least two hairdressers, a tattoo shop and a flower shop. The flower shop is my favourite shop in the town. The woman has a white plastic bag and there's not much in it, so it's likely that she has just been to one of the bakers or somewhere else to make a small purchase. It's also possible that she hasn't been to a shop at all and the bag contains something else. All of it is pure speculation.

woman with a shopping bag. She wearing heels to go to the shop. Although she's walking up the hill so she probably coming back from the shop

WOMAN WITH SHOPPING BAG/FRAU MIT EINKAUFSTASCHE

I bought a rose tree. I bought a rose. I bought a red rose. I bought a white rose. I bought a rose that was pink. The rose tree was red and was called a true love rose. I bought a rose tree. I bought a rose. I bought a red rose. I bought a white rose. I bought a rose that was pink. The rose tree was red and was called a true love rose. I bought a rose tree. I bought a rose. I bought a red rose. I bought a white rose. I bought a rose that was pink. The rose tree was red and was called a true love rose. I bought a rose tree. I bought a rose. I bought a red rose. I bought a white rose. I bought a rose that was pink. The rose tree was red and was called a true love rose. I bought a rose tree. I bought a rose. I bought a red rose. I bought a white rose. I bought a rose that was pink. The rose tree was red and was called a true love rose. I bought a rose tree. I bought a rose. I bought a red rose. I bought a white rose. I bought a rose that was pink. The rose tree was red and was called a true love rose. I bought a rose tree. I bought a rose. I bought a red rose. I bought a white rose. I bought a rose that was pink. The rose tree was red and was called a true love rose. I bought a rose tree. I bought a rose. I bought a red rose. I bought a white rose. I bought a rose that was pink. The rose tree was red and was called a true love rose. I bought a rose tree. I bought a rose. I bought a red rose. I bought a white rose. I bought a rose that was pink. The rose tree was red and was called a true love rose. I bought a rose tree. I bought a rose. I bought a red rose. I bought a white rose. I bought a rose that

was pink. The rose tree was red and was called a true love rose. I bought a rose tree. I bought a rose. I bought a red rose. I bought a white rose. I bought a rose that was pink. The rose tree was red and was called a true love rose. I bought a rose tree. I bought a rose. I bought a red rose. I bought a white rose. I bought a rose that was pink. The rose tree was red and was called a true love rose. I bought a rose tree. I bought a rose. I bought a red rose. I bought a white rose. I bought a rose that was pink. The rose tree was red and was called a true love rose. I bought a rose tree. I bought a rose. I bought a red rose. I bought a white rose. I bought a rose that was pink. The rose tree was red and was called a true love rose. I bought a rose tree. I bought a rose. I bought a red rose. I bought a white rose. I bought a rose that was pink. The rose tree was red and was called a true love rose. I bought a rose tree. I bought a rose. I bought a red rose. I bought a white rose. I bought a rose that was pink. The rose tree was red and was called a true love rose. I bought a rose tree. I bought a rose. I bought a red rose. I bought a white rose. I bought a rose that was pink. The rose tree was red and was called a true love rose. I bought a rose tree. I bought a rose. I bought a red rose. I bought a white rose. I bought a rose that was pink. The rose tree was red and was called a true love rose. I bought a rose tree. I bought a rose. I bought a red rose. I bought a white rose. I bought a rose that was pink. The rose tree was red and was called a true love rose. I bought a rose tree. I bought a rose. I bought a red rose. I bought a white rose. I bought a rose that was pink. The rose tree was red and was called a true love rose. I bought a rose tree. I bought a rose. I

SILVER CAR TURNING CORNER/
SILBERNES AUTO FÄHRT UM DIE ECKE

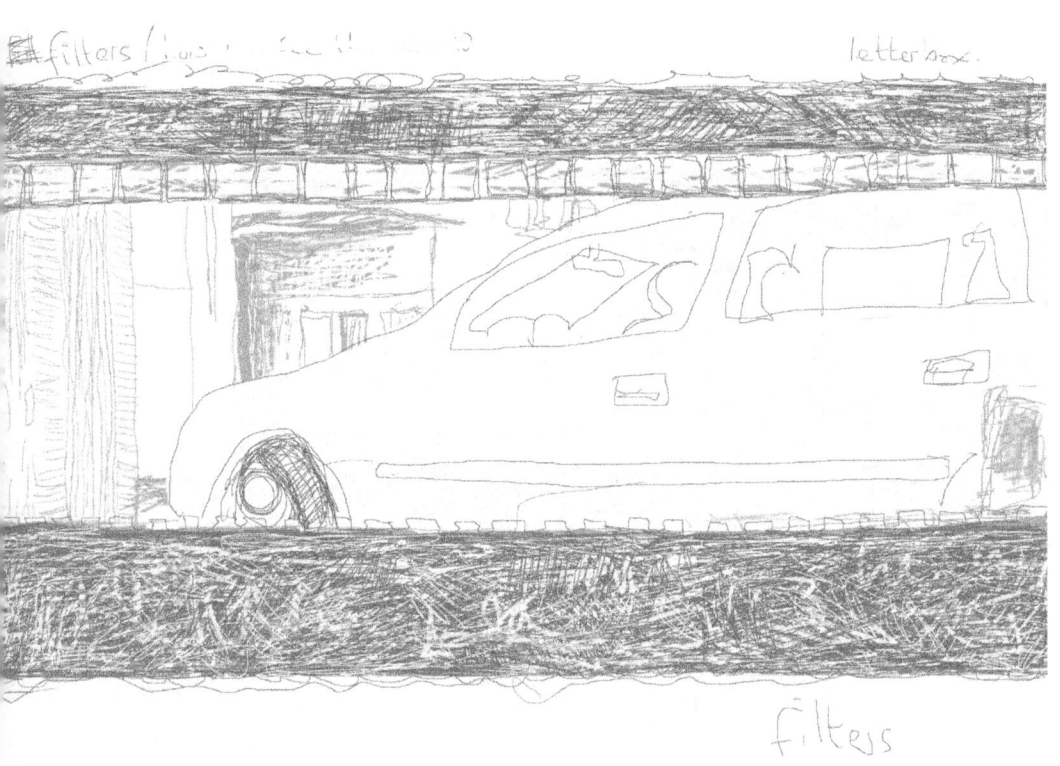

filters / ... letterbox.

filters

**SILVER CAR TURNING CORNER/
SILBERNES AUTO FÄHRT UM DIE ECKE**

turning a corner

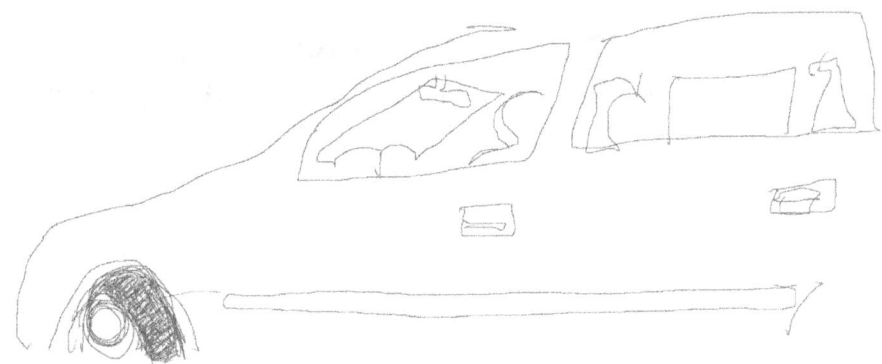

~~both literally and figuratively~~ ~~the~~ most of the
where the car obscures ~~the~~ ~~the~~ image.
It's not the turning of the corner that obscures but the
closeness to the editing flap [letterbox].
pressure and obscuring

**SILVER CAR TURNING CORNER/
SILBERNES AUTO FÄHRT UM DIE ECKE**

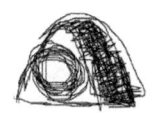

edit things down to the most basic
elements required to turn a
corner.
To turn a corner all you need
is a wheel. Even these words
are unnecessary.

**SILVER CAR TURNING CORNER/
SILBERNES AUTO FÄHRT UM DIE ECKE**

Extend

obscure

Erase

There are consequences to including information.

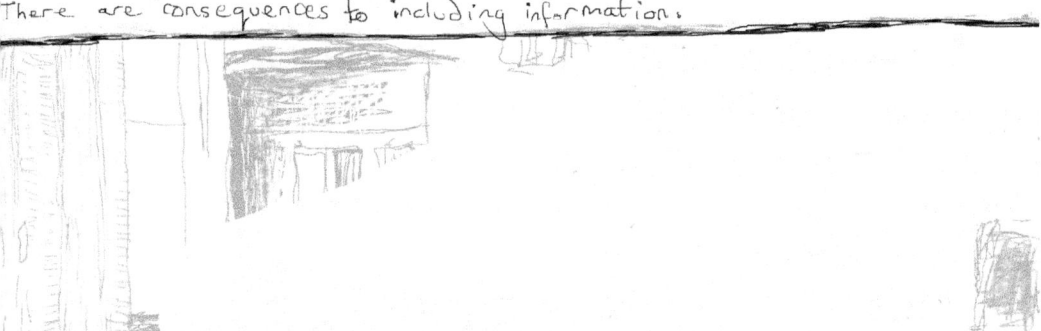

- nothing from the original image
  (I have broken this in relation to arts)
  Katzen

- no identifying features of individuals
  (I have been very strict about this)

- nothing leading to the identification
  of an individual
  (I have been mostly strict about this)

There are consequences to including everything so it
is necessary to extend, obscure, erase.
edited out. obscured . erased.

**SILVER CAR TURNING CORNER/
SILBERNES AUTO FÄHRT UM DIE ECKE**

What if all of the informaiton is put back in? What if the editing process is entirely additive instead of reductive? What if the result of the editing process is the original plus lots of extra information, such as context. Does each iteration increase the amount of information? The only thing that's missing is the original image. What if all of the informaiton is put back in? What if the editing process is entirely additive instead of reductive? What if the result of the editing process is the original plus lots of extra information, such as context. Does each iteration increase the amount of information? The only thing that's missing is the original image. What if all of the informaiton is put back in? What if the editing process is entirely additive instead of reductive? What if the result of the editing process is the original plus lots of extra information, such as context. Does each iteration increase the amount of information? The only thing that's missing is the original image. What if all of the informaiton is put back in? What if the editing process is entirely additive instead of reductive? What if the result of the editing process is the original plus lots of extra information, such as context. Does each iteration increase the amount of information? The only thing that's missing is the original image. What if all of the informaiton is put back in? What if the editing process is entirely additive instead of reductive? What if the result of the editing process is the original plus lots of extra information, such as context. Does each iteration increase the amount of information?

What if all of the informaiton is put back in? What if the editing process is entirely additive instead of reductive? What if the result of the editing process is the original plus lots of extra information, such as context. Does each iteration increase the amount of information? The only thing that's missing is the original image. What if all of the informaiton is put back in? What if the editing process is entirely additive instead of reductive? What if the result of the editing process is the original plus lots of extra information, such as context. Does each iteration increase the amount of information? The only thing that's missing is the original image. What if all of the informaiton is put back in? What if the editing process is entirely additive instead of reductive? What if the result of the editing process is the original plus lots of extra information, such as context. Does each iteration increase the amount of information? The only thing that's missing is the original image. What if all of the informaiton is put back in? What if the editing process is entirely additive instead of reductive? What if the result of the editing process is the original plus lots of extra information, such as context. Does each iteration increase the amount of information? The only thing that's missing is the original image. What if all of the informaiton is put back in? What if the editing process is entirely additive instead of reductive? What if the result of the editing process is the original plus lots of extra information, such as context. Does each iteration increase the amount of information?

WOMAN WITH BLUE BAG/FRAU MIT BLAUER TASCHE

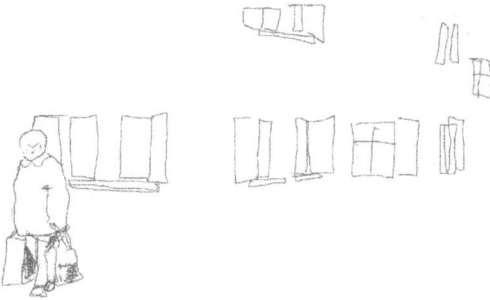

WOMAN WITH BLUE BAG/FRAU MIT BLAUER TASCHE

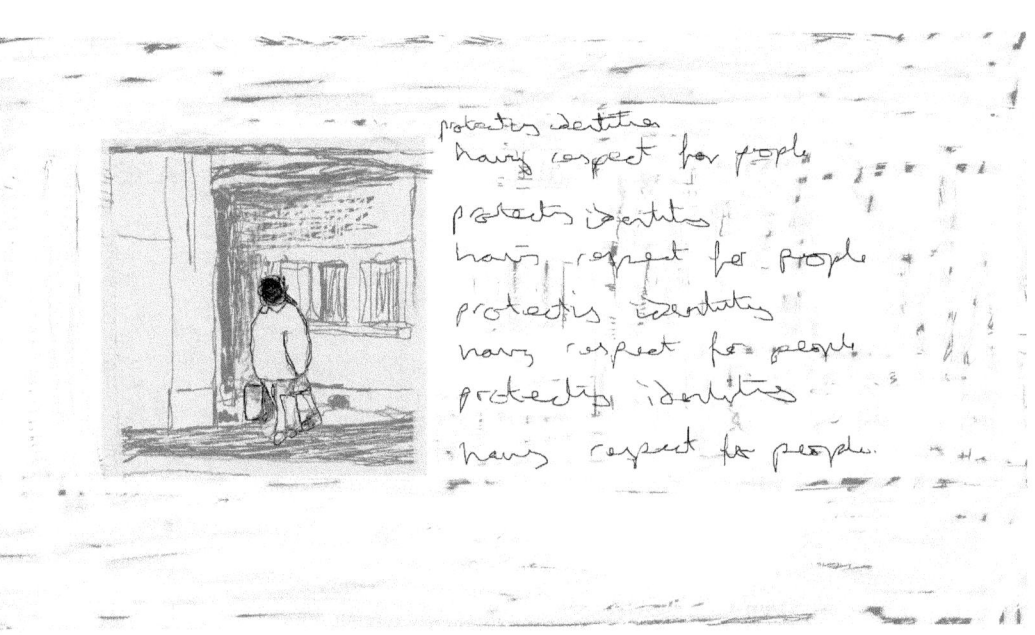

protecting identities
having respect for people

protecting identities
having respect for people

protecting identities
having respect for people

protecting identities
having respect for people

WOMAN WITH BLUE BAG/FRAU MIT BLAUER TASCHE

people leave
an indelible
stain on
things sometimes

people leave an indelible
stain on things
sometimes

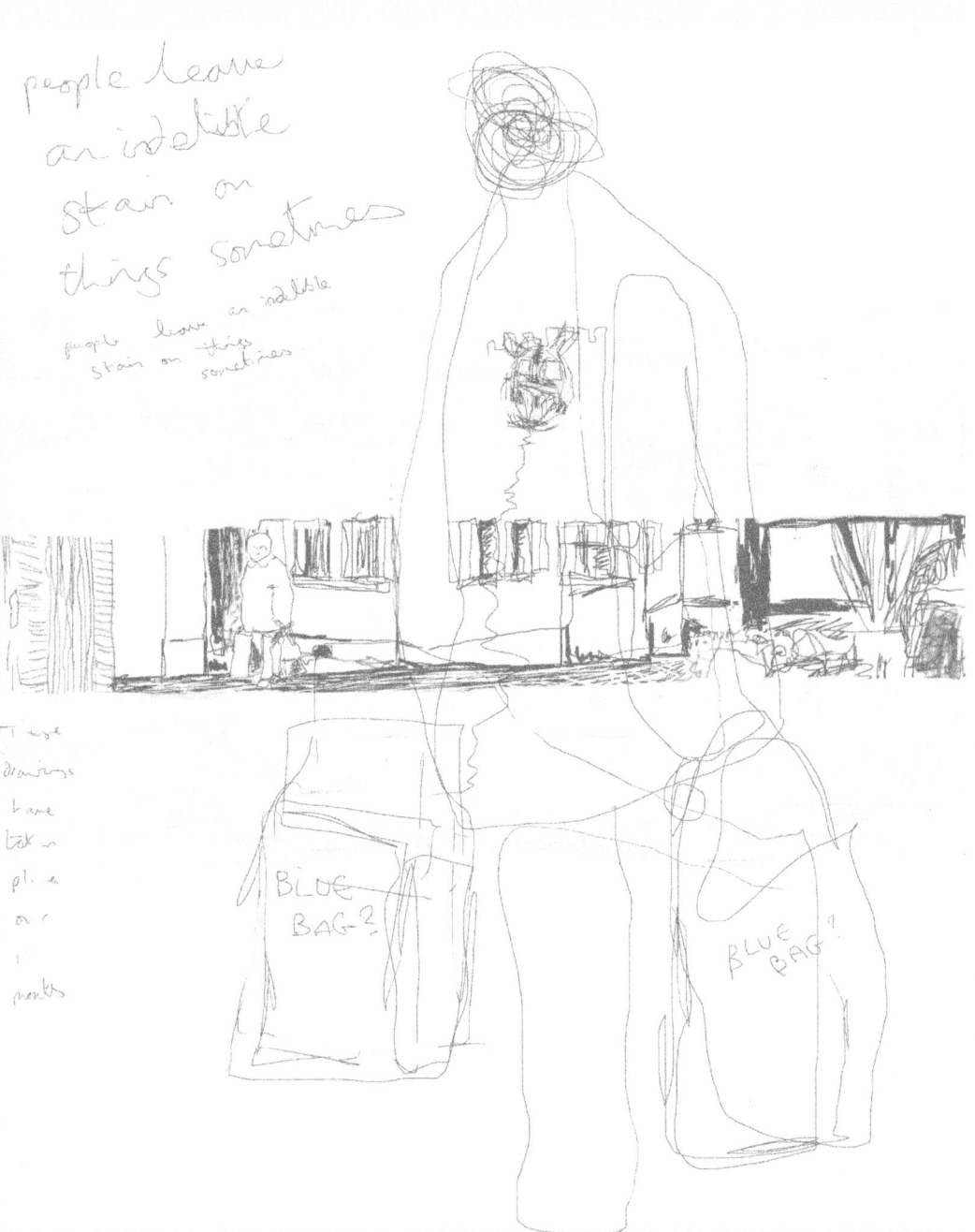

BLUE
BAG?

BLUE
BAG?

MAN IN BLUE TRAINERS/MANN MIT BLAUEN TURNSCHUHEN

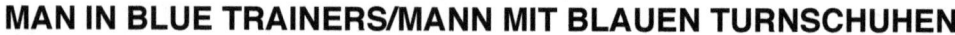

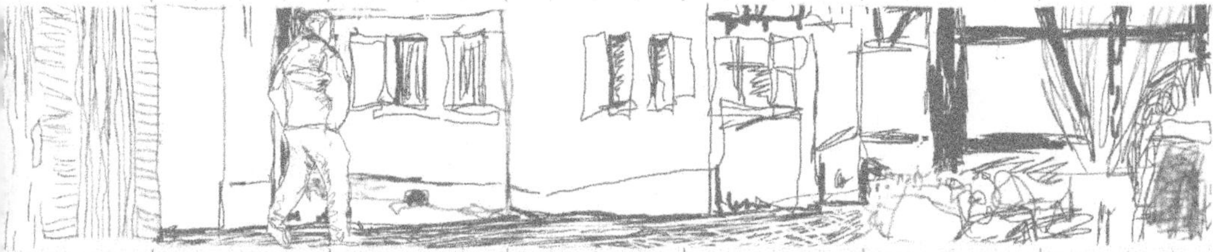

MAN IN BLUE TRAINERS/MANN MIT BLAUEN TURNSCHUHEN

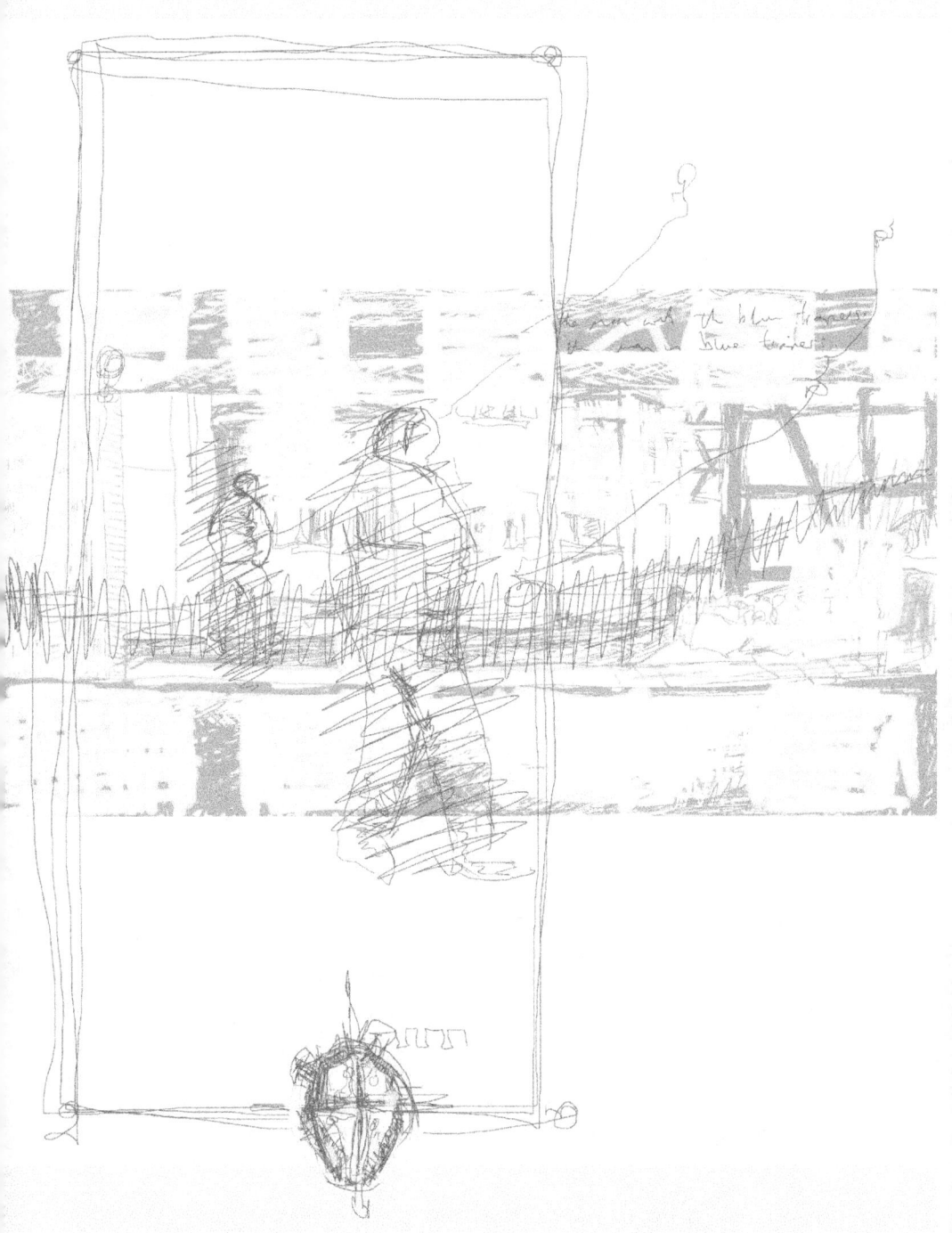

MAN IN BLUE TRAINERS/MANN MIT BLAUEN TURNSCHUHEN

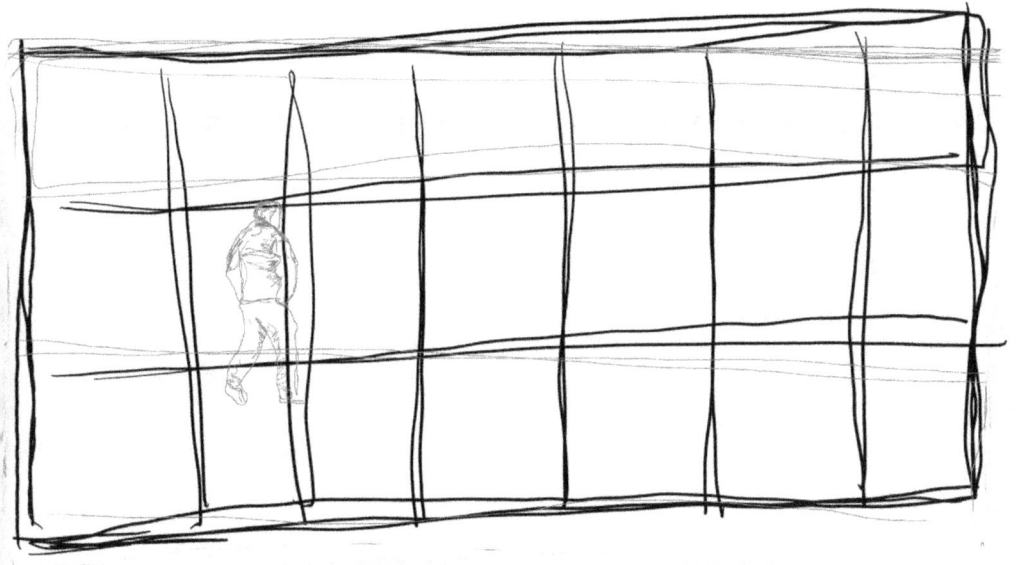

MAN IN BLUE TRAINERS/MANN MIT BLAUEN TURNSCHUHEN

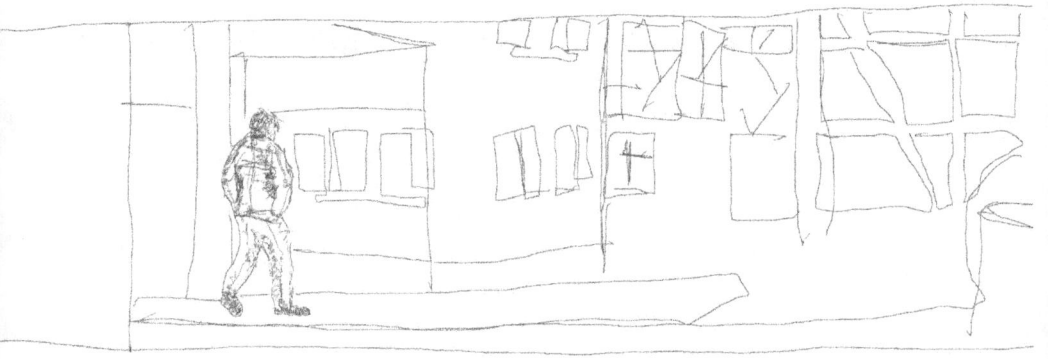

MAN IN BLUE TRAINERS/MANN MIT BLAUEN TURNSCHUHEN

A fixed perspective can be a way to achieve depth while considering one subject. I have always been rather conceptually promiscuous but I have the ability to focus on one subject until I have completely exhausted it. This particular book has been in development for an extended period of time. For this reason, it takes into account many different influences and perspectives while remaining true to the subject matter that was recorded on 38th March 2015.

This man I know very slightly. I have spoken to him maybe four or five times in the two and a half years that I've lived in Niederbrechen. I know his name, where he lives and his family set up, how long he's been in Germany and that's it. I think that I know more about him than he knows about me.

CAR WITH REFLECTED LIGHTS/
AUTO MIT REFLEKTIERTEM LICHT

point of resistance

CAR WITH REFLECTED LIGHTS/
AUTO MIT REFLEKTIERTEM LICHT

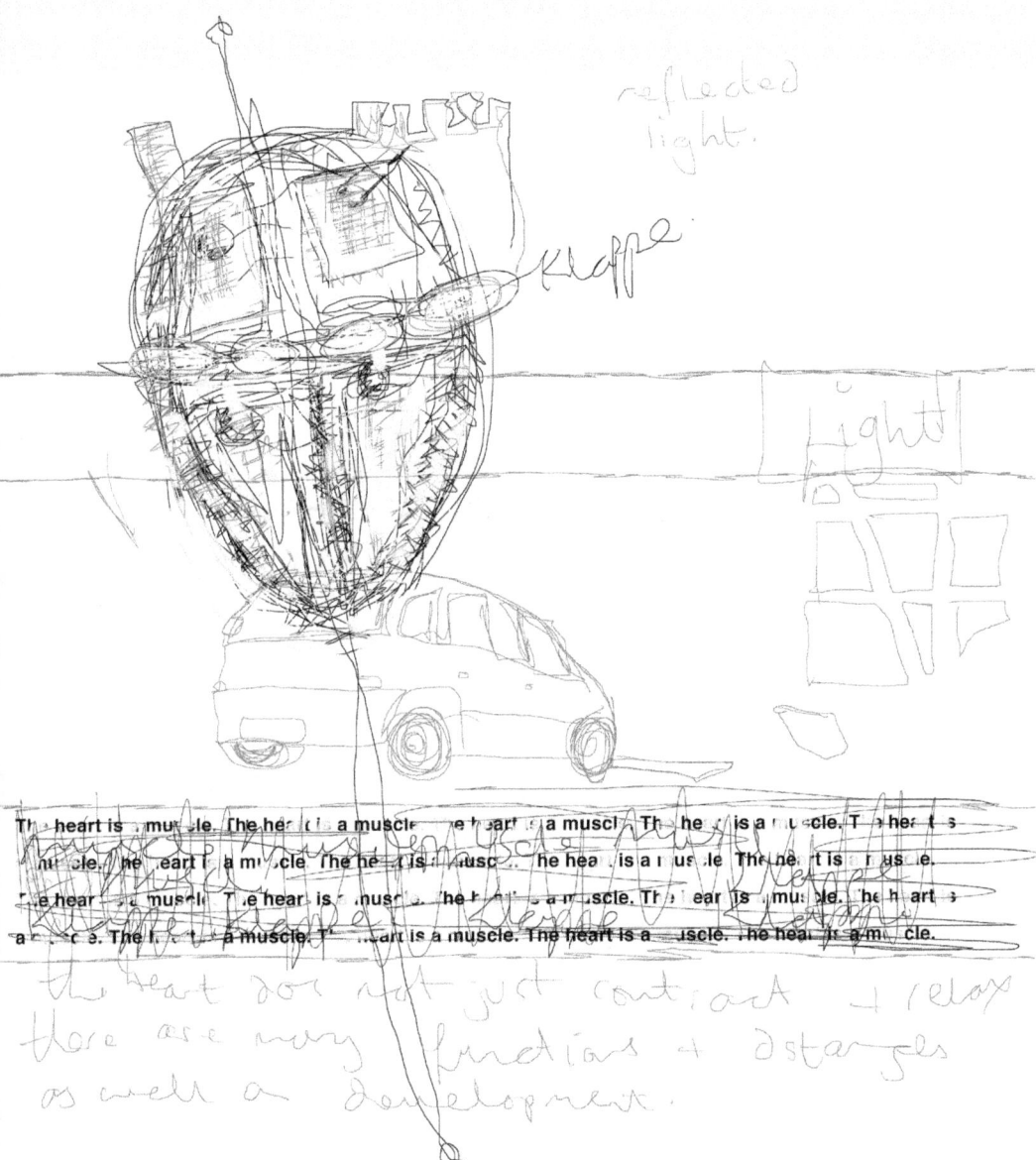

reflected light.

klappe

Light

The heart is a muscle. The heart is a muscle.

the heart does not just contract + relax there are many functions + discharges as well a development.

CAR WITH REFLECTED LIGHTS/
AUTO MIT REFLEKTIERTEM LICHT

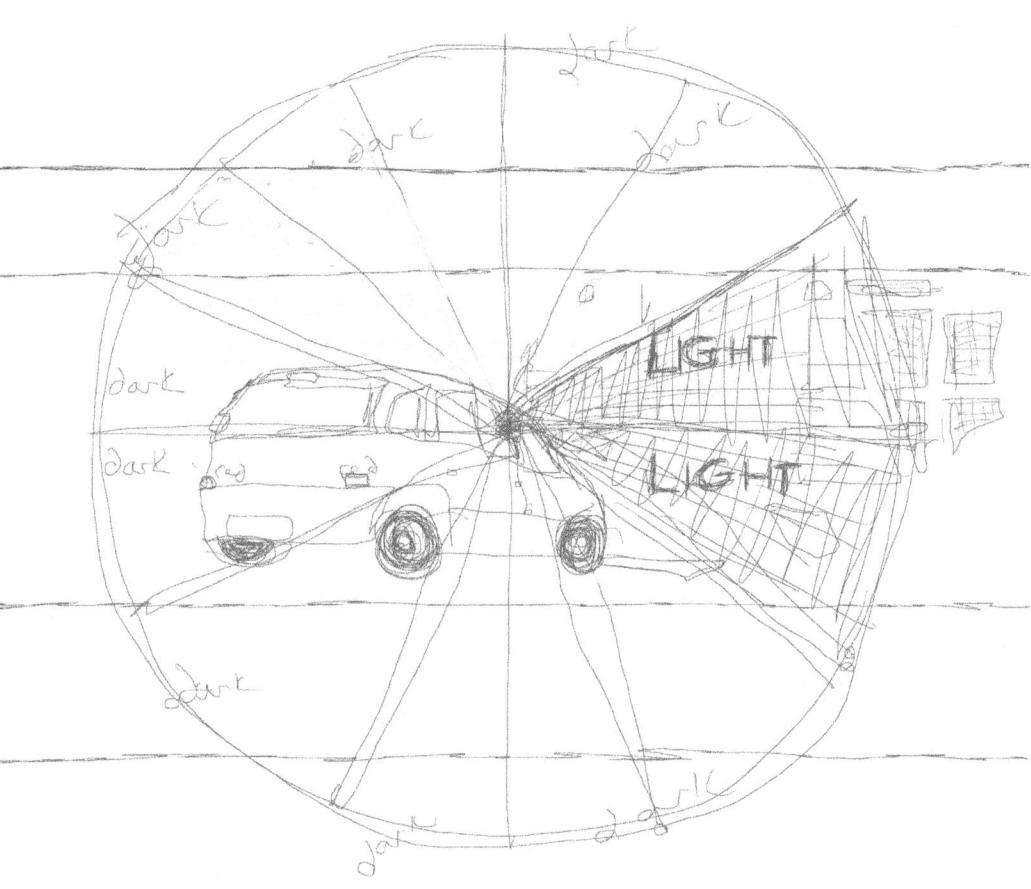

CAR WITH REFLECTED LIGHTS/
AUTO MIT REFLEKTIERTEM LICHT

How do you get to the point of
resistance? Does unification happen
before or after this point?
... the point of resistance be
...

How do you get to the point of
resistance?

How do you get to the point of
resistance? It takes a lot of strength.

LIGHT

**CAR WITH REFLECTED LIGHTS/
AUTO MIT REFLEKTIERTEM LICHT**

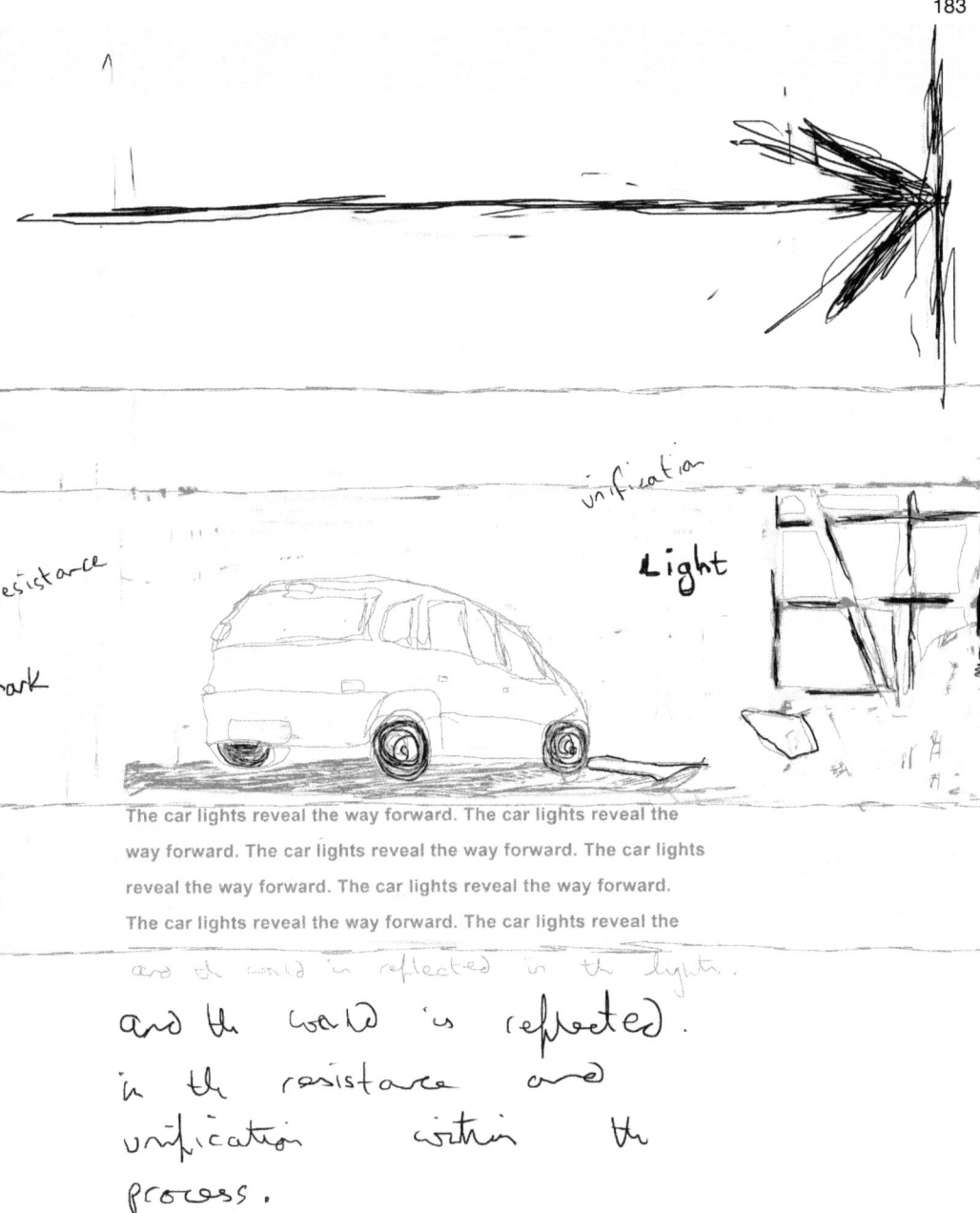

resistance

dark

unification

Light

The car lights reveal the way forward. The car lights reveal the way forward. The car lights reveal the way forward. The car lights reveal the way forward. The car lights reveal the way forward. The car lights reveal the way forward. The car lights reveal the

and the world is reflected in the lights.

and the world is reflected. in the resistance and unification within the process.

BLACK AND WHITE CAT/SCHWARZ-WEISSE KATZE

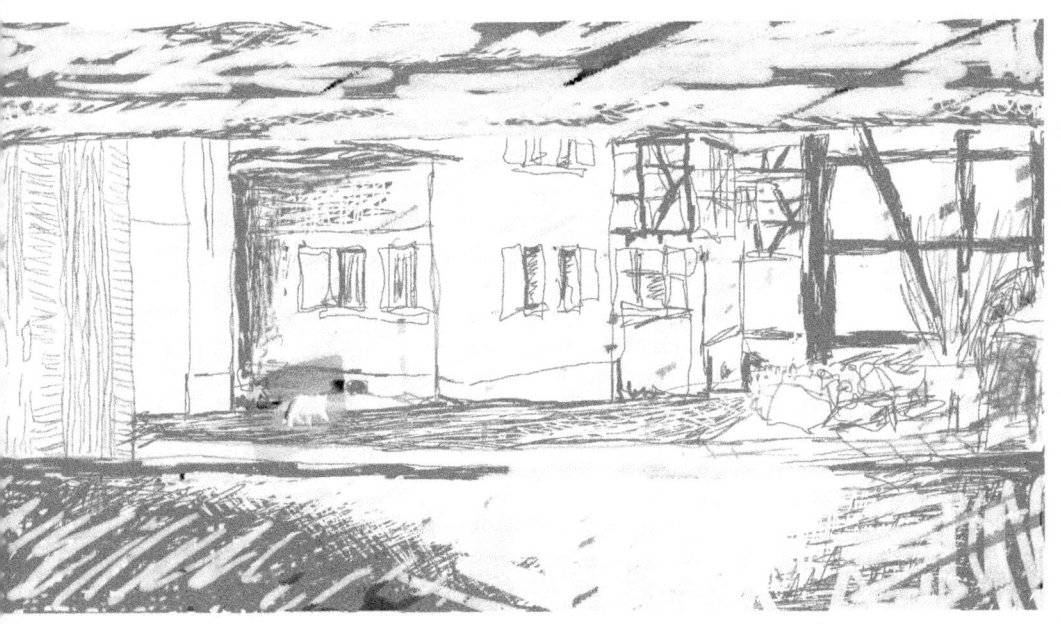

BLACK AND WHITE CAT/SCHWARZ-WEISSE KATZE

The black and white cat
has moved away now.

BLACK AND WHITE CAT/SCHWARZ-WEISSE KATZE

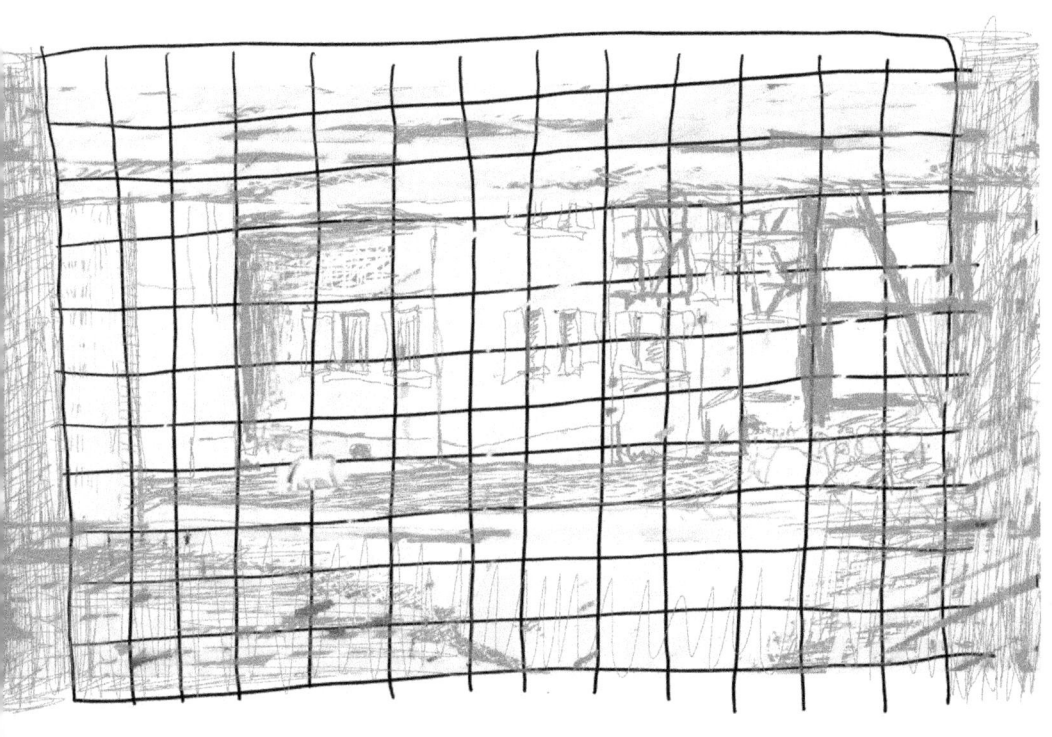

don't go, putty. stay with me.

BLACK AND WHITE CAT/SCHWARZ-WEISSE KATZE

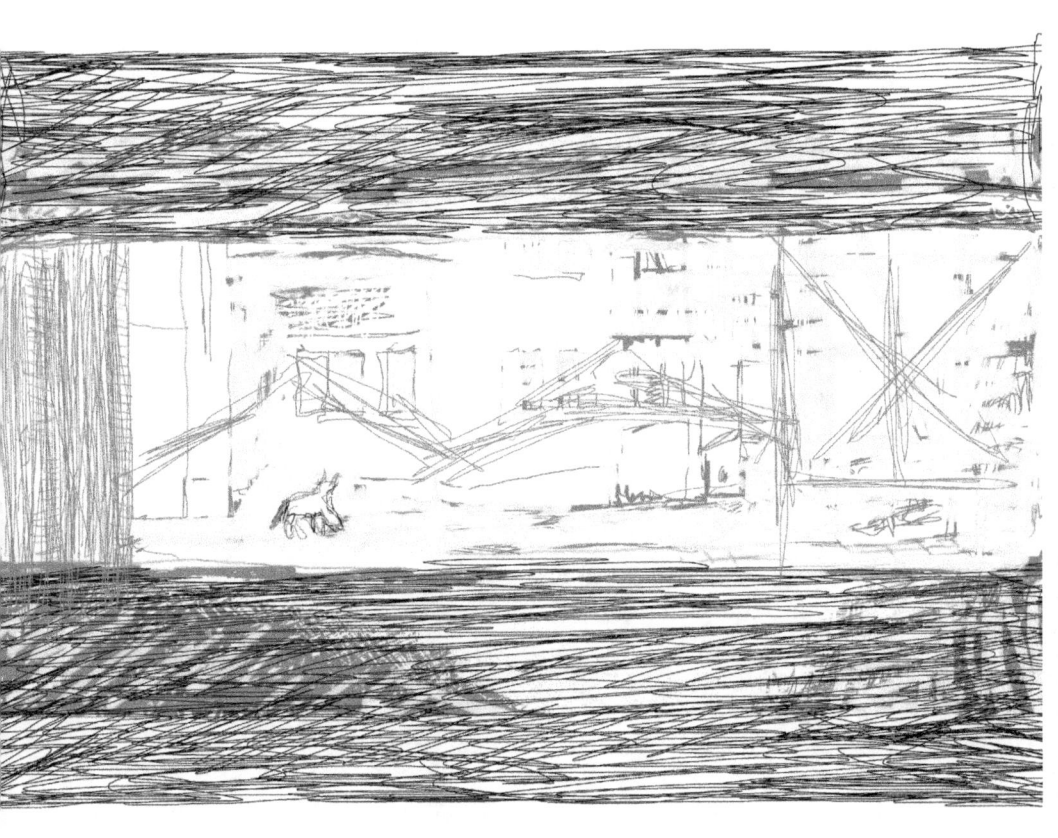

Black + white cat.

Katze

Katze

RED CAR/ROTES AUTO

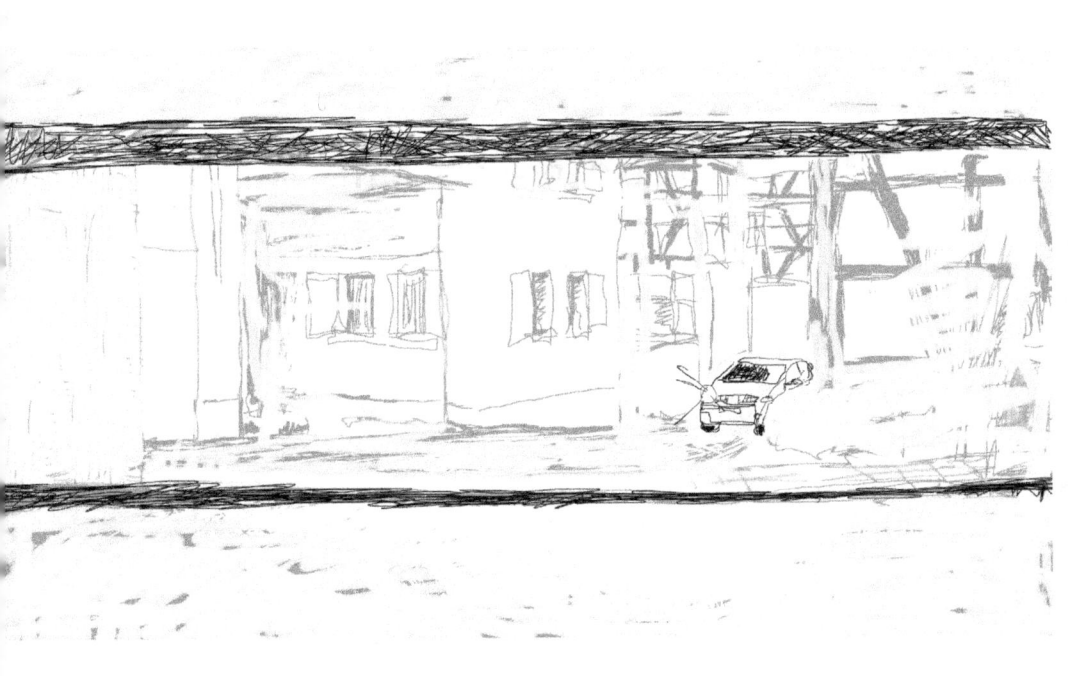

RED CAR/ROTES AUTO

This is a red car. This is not a red car.

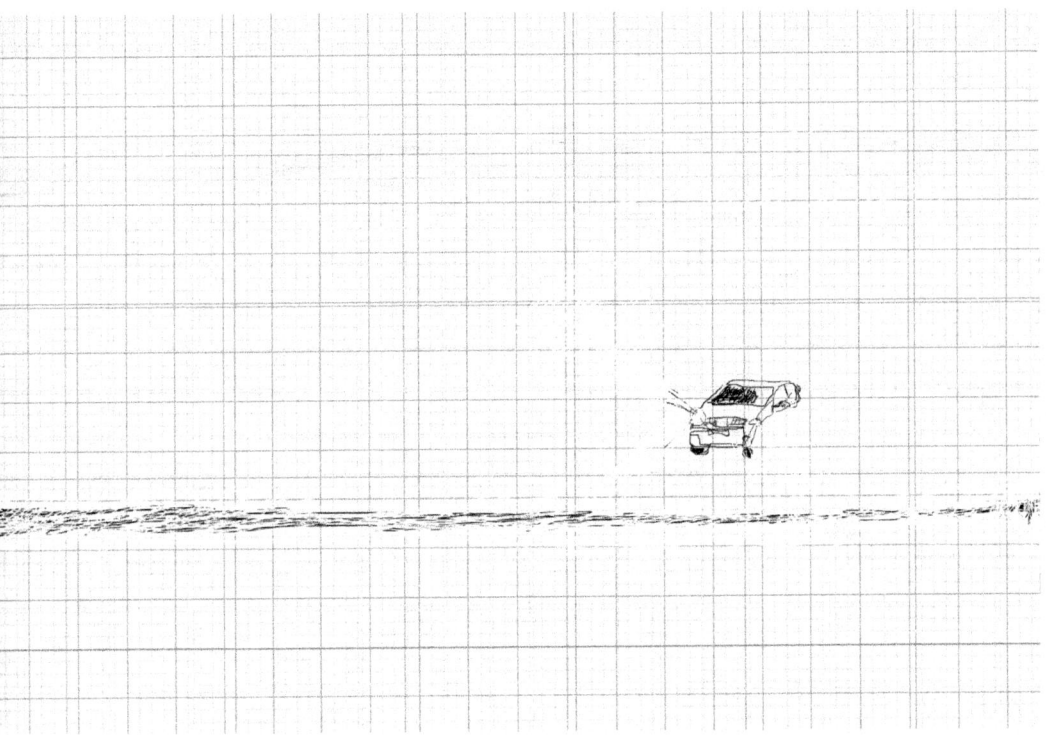

This is a **red car**. But at the same time this is not a red car. The fact that this is not a colour publication is a highly political matter. It relates to economics on a wide scale and more specifically the status of the artist and how the work of artists is valued (or not valued) in society. I am not saying that I think it should be the opposite of how it is now, that every mark made by an artist should have value, but it is an important issue and there should be balance in it. There is no balance in the current system. Some individuals sell their work for large amounts of money and many artists are left without basic resources. A colour publication is not a basic resource, although I disagree that making art is a luxury in itself because it can create hardship. However, a colour publication would result in a vastly increased cost of production and resale, which would exclude many people who might be interested in owning a copy of this work. The increased production costs would indicate that the basic needs have been met and that there is a surplus. Currently there is no surplus and in the past the basic needs have definitely not been met. The colour of this car remains an ongoing political matter. If the individual circumstances of the artist change then the car may remain not red, for principle's sake.

RED CAR/ROTES AUTO

red car red car red car red car red car red car red car
red car red car red car red car red car red car red car
red car red car red car red car red car red car red car
red car red car red car red car red car red car red car
red car red car red car red car red car red car red car
red car red car red car red car red car red car red car
red car red car red car red car red car red car red car
red car red car red car red car red car red car red car
red car red car red car red car red car red car red car
red car red car red car red car red car red car red car
red car red car red car red car red car red car red car
red car red car red car red car red car red car red car
red car red car red car red car red car red car red car
red car red car red car red car red car red car red car
red car red car red car red car red car red car red car
red car red car red car red car red car red car red car

This is a red car. This is also a red car.

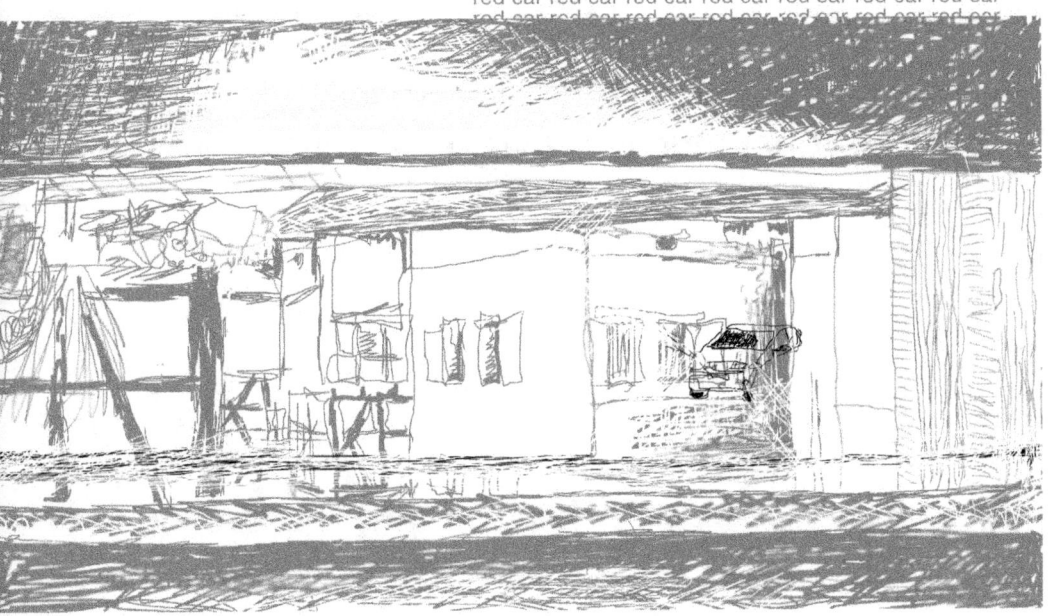

red car. red car.

colour

society. I am

A colour

colour

colour

car red.

CHANGING LIGHT/WECHSELNDES LICHT

The erasure of personal experiences.

The erasure of personal experiences by others because they upset their delicate sensibilities. This is a class issue. Being expected to erase my history in order to not disrupt others status quo results in them having — maintaining — power and me having none. No history, no contribution. This week, 3rd week of August 2016, someone actually implied that I had imagined my experiences [different perceptions...]. This goes beyond erasure and into a re-editing where my experiences are re-written as not real. ~~not~~ With erasure my previous life is also hidden from view and not ~~cast~~ as imaginary. But it is all very real, and shouldn't be re-written or hidden — erased or reimagined. I have a contribution to make and it may not fit other's idea of their comfortable little world but it remains a contribution none the less.

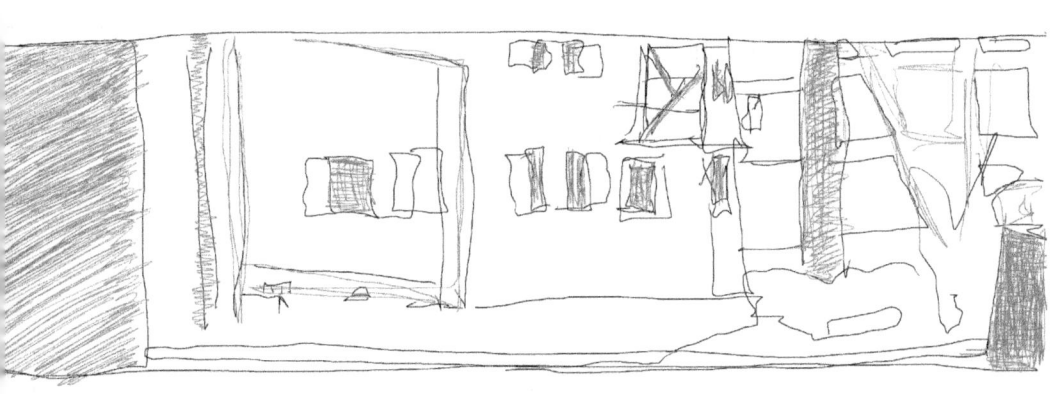

However,
~~this~~ this is a class issue but it comes from British and American people. I have not experienced this from any German people and in general, very generally, they seem considerably more open-minded and less judgemental. So it's a British/American class issue and not a cultural issue. Eventually, I can remove myself completely from these ~~day to day~~ day to day things that have such a huge impact. By reclaiming power and insisting that I have a contribution and will not be erased. I own my history.

changing light — shining a light
on an issue.

CHANGING LIGHT/WECHSELNDES LICHT

changing light .

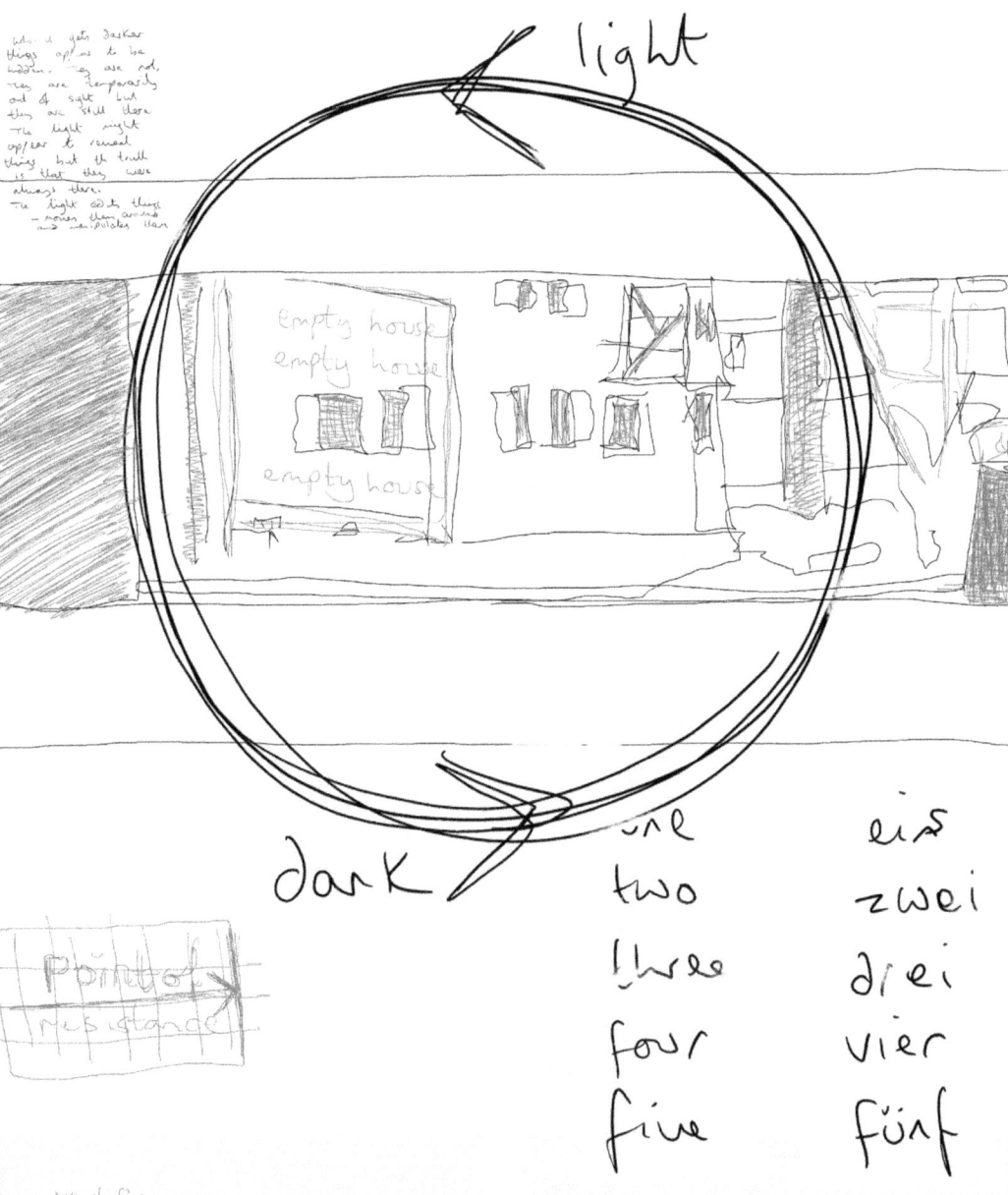

When it gets darker things appear to be hidden. They are not, they are temporarily out of sight but they are still there. The light might appear to reveal things but the truth is that they were always there. The light edits things - moves them around and manipulates them

light

empty house
empty house

empty house

dark

Point of
resistance

one   eis
two   zwei
three   drei
four   vier
five   fünf

one of five

CHANGING LIGHT/WECHSELNDES LICHT

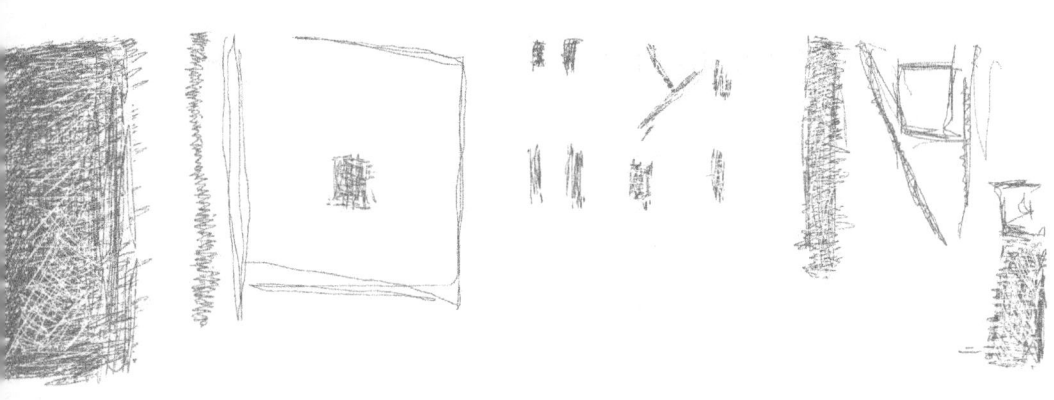

CHANGING LIGHT/WECHSELNDES LICHT

The erasure of experiences.

erasure leads to the point of resistance.

erasure leads to the point of resistance

erasure of events a re-editing the past.

The erasure of events

A re-editing of the past

one of the reasons
This is why Frankfurt reminds me of Liverpool. There is ownership of the past and terrible things that (In Frankfurt's case across the whole of Germany) have happened, but at the same time looking to the FUTURE. London isn't like that because its too busy (treading water) just trying to exist in the present.

one of five

CHANGING LIGHT/WECHSELNDES LICHT

The erasure of experiences.
The erasure of events
The editing of experiences
The editing of events.

UNIFICATION

EDITING/
ERASURE

Point of acceptance
resistance

Point of
resistance

The editing of events
not to manipulate but to
reveal other histories.

changing light

BIOGRAPHY

Kate Pelling is a British artist based in Germany. Her transdisciplinary research-led practice consists mainly of experimental video, drawing and text. Kate Pelling studied at Wirral Metropolitan College, Birkenhead (2003), Wimbledon School of Art, London (2004), Birkbeck, University of London (2008) and Chelsea College of Arts, University of the Arts London (2016). She has exhibited extensively in the UK and the USA, and also in Bulgaria, Canada, Germany, Italy, Lithuania, Portugal, and Switzerland. Kate Pelling's previous publications, *A Relational [Video] Grammar: Extrapolation* (2013) and *[Video] Klappe* (2014) are also published by Fifth Floor Publications.

BIOGRAFIE

Kate Pelling ist eine in Deutschland lebende britische Künstlerin. Ihre transdisziplinäre forschungsgeleitete Arbeit umfasst hauptsächlich experimentelles Video, Zeichnen und Text. Kate Pelling studierte am Wirral Metropolitan College, Birkenhead (2003), an der Wimbledon School of Art, London (2004), Birkbeck, University of London (2008) und am Chelsea College of Arts, University of the Arts London (2016). Ihre Werke wurden in großen Ausstellungen in Großbritannien und den USA sowie Bulgarien, Kanada, Deutschland, Italien, Litauen, Portugal und der Schweiz ausgestellt. Kate Pellings frühere Bücher, *A Relational [Video] Grammar: Extrapolation* (2013) und *[Video] Klappe* (2014) werden ebenfalls von Fifth Floor Publications veröffentlicht.

ACKNOWLEDGEMENTS

Thank you to Martin Peter for translating the text of this publication.

I would like to thank Nathan Evans, Paul Ryan, Otelo M Fabião, Hazel Pelling, Aaron McPeake, Becca Permar and Jim Irvin's voice for their continuing support in every area of my life and work. Special thanks goes to Britta Färber and Christina März for their support and encouragement over the last year.

To my muse, who will be leaving me at the end of this year – thank you for everything, you are wonderful and I will miss you.

This publication is dedicated to the memory of my brothers, John and Stuart Pelling.

DANKSAGUNGEN

Danke an Martin Peter für die Übersetzung des Textes dieses Buches.

Ich möchte mich bei Nathan Evans, Paul Ryan, Otelo M Fabião, Hazel Pelling, Aaron McPeake, Becca Permar und Jim Irvins Stimme für ihre langjährige Hilfe in allen Bereichen meines Lebens und Schaffens bedanken. Besonderer Dank an Britta Färber und Christina März für ihre Unterstützung und dafür, dass sie mich im vergangenen Jahr immer wieder ermutigt haben.

An meine Muse, die mich Ende des Jahres verlassen wird - ich danke Dir für alles, Du bist wunderbar und ich werde Dich vermissen.

Dieses Werk ist dem Andenken meiner Brüder John und Stuart Pelling gewidmet.

FIFTH FLOOR PUBLICATIONS

Fifth Floor Publications was founded in 2012 and is based in London, UK and Frankfurt am Main, Germany. Fifth Floor Publications is a publisher of artists' books that use transdisciplinary methods, with an emphasis on experimental works that examine aspects of making artists' film and video or drawing practices.

Previously published titles include *A Relational [Video] Grammar: Extrapolation* by Kate Pelling (2013) and *[Video] Klappe* by Kate Pelling (2014).

FIFTH FLOOR PUBLICATIONS

Fifth Floor Publications wurde im Jahre 2012 gegründet und hat ihren Sitz in London, Großbritannien und Frankfurt am Main, Deutschland. Fifth Floor Publications ist ein Verlag für Künstlerbücher, die transdisziplinäre Methoden einsetzen, mit Schwerpunkt auf experimentellen Werken, die Aspekte der Schaffung von Künstlerfilmen, Video und Zeichnungspraktiken untersuchen.

Unter den bereits veröffentlichten Titeln sind *A Relational [Video] Grammar: Extrapolation* von Kate Pelling (2013) und *[Video] Klappe* von Kate Pelling (2014).